C000205364

The Simplicity of Dressage

The Simplicity of Dressage

Claartje van Andel

Johann Hinnemann & Coby van Baalen

Translated by Marji Mc Fadden, M.A.

J. A. Allen

First published in the English language in the United States of America
by Trafalgar Square Publishing in 2003

This edition published in Great Britain in 2003

J.A. Allen
Clerkenwell House
Clerkenwell Green
London EC1R 0HT

J.A. Allen is an imprint of Robert Hale Ltd.

Originally published in the Dutch language as *De eenvoud van de dressuur*
by Fontaine Uitgevers, Abcoude, 2002

ISBN: 0 85131 891 6

A catalogue record for this book is available from the British Library

Design and typographical editing by Hans Lodewijkx and Linda van Eijndhoven

Printed in Hong Kong

Contents

Johann Hinnemann on Ribot and Coby van Baalen on Commodore. They placed first and second in the 1992 Grand Prix at Cologne.

Preface

The first time that Johann Hinnemann came to my home in Brakel, Belgium, he opened my storage closet and asked if I had a museum in my home. He saw bits and spurs in various shapes and sizes. I thought that I needed everything that hung there! If he opens this storage closet now, it really is a museum. I no longer use anything special in my training, for when I began training with Johann Hinnemann more than ten years ago, I discovered simplicity.

This book is about the simplicity of dressage, not because dressage is so simple to do, but because all dressage theory always comes down to the same basic principles. Ultimately, dressage is simple to explain: whether you are dealing with a three-year-old horse or a seasoned schoolmaster, the training basics are fundamentally the same.

That is reassuring for anyone who is continually trying to understand a new horse, to school him, and possibly to show him. Even with new horses, the training basics always come down to working on and perfecting the six central basic concepts. These are rhythm, *losgelassenheit* (relaxation), contact, impulsion, straightness, and collection.

We have thoroughly enjoyed working on this book. We have also resisted the temptation to make it a more extensive book, for are we not writing that dressage is ultimately simple? We have many more good examples, and we could have given many more anecdotes with specific stories about our horses, enough to fill another book. Perhaps we will still do that later, but all these stories would have distracted us from our present topic: A clear summary of horse training; the six basic concepts; and simplicity. And simplicity is what we want to emphasize in this book.

We hope that you enjoy reading this book and that you subsequently enjoy it more in practice. Your horse will reward you for the logic and simplicity in your training.

Brakel/Voerde, September 2002

Also on behalf of Johann Hinnemann,
Coby van Baalen

Introduction

Johann Hinnemann (August 29, 1948)
Johann Hinnemann is one of the best known and most sought after dressage trainers in the world. Just like every farmer's son who starts riding horses, Jo's interest did not begin with dressage but with the all-around work on the land. From 1968-1972, he did his professional rider training in Münster, where the late Dr. Reiner Klimke, the former Olympic champion, resided. In addition to Dr. Klimke, Johann learned a great deal from Günter Guminski.

In 1972, Johann married his wife Gisela, and in that year, he took over Krüsterhof, located in Voerde, Germany on the lower Rhein. He developed the property into a breeding and boarding facility with a riding school. Gisela and Johann had a son and a daughter, Stephan and Bettina.

In 1976, Johann passed the professional exam for riding instructors (Berufsreitlehrerprüfung). In 1978, he became the Rheinland champion with Duero and received the golden Rider's Pin (golden Reiterabzeichen). In 1980, he earned high scores at Grand Prix with Genius.

In those years, Johann Hinnemann also devoted himself to the rights of professionals in international sports. At that time, professional trainers were still forbidden from participating in international championships. That changed through his lobbying efforts. In 1986, Johann Hinnemann won the team gold and individual bronze medals at the Dressage World Championships in Cedar Valley, Canada. A year later, in 1987, he won the team gold and individual bronze medals at the European Dressage Championships at Goodwood. His constant partner in winning these medals was the Dutch bred horse, Ideaal. Then and still now, Hinnemann can count on the expert support of Albert Stecken.

Hinnemann bases his successful equestrian career on being professionally goal-oriented and having the courage to confidently follow his own path. He also tries to impart these qualities to his students and to his horses.

In 1996, Johann Hinnemann was awarded the rarely bestowed title of Reitmeister (Master Rider).

Johann Hinnemann is also very involved with breeding. He expanded his facility with a separate mare barn and a breeding station. In 1999, he became the stallion trainer for the Nordrhein-Westfälisches Landgestüt, the National Stud Farm in Warendorf.

For many years, Hinnemann was the team trainer for Canada. In 1997 and 1998, he was the national coach for the German team, together with Klaus Balkenhol.

The 2000 Olympic Games in Sydney were very memorable for Johann Hinnemann. When the medals for international dressage were being awarded, he could delight in his contribution to every medal winner's career. His student Alexandra Simons-de Ridder was part of the gold-winning German team. Coby van Baalen had a part in the silver medal for the Netherlands. Finally, Christine Traurig contributed to the American bronze medal team.

The Dutch rider Coby van Baalen is his most loyal student, along with her daughter, Marlies.

Coby van Baalen (April 6, 1957)
Coby Dorresteijn, a farmer's daughter, taught gymnastics to neighborhood children at the young age of seven, and wrote motivational texts in a notebook, suggesting that the children had done their best, but they needed to keep practicing. With that in mind, it is surprising that Coby did not dedicate herself to writing a book on dressage training sooner!

Coby had to fight for her first horse. There were years on the farm when money was earned from their cows and the fruit they grew. A favorite saying of Coby's father, Jan Dorresteijn, was, "If you want to eat dry bread, then you should have horses." However, Coby persisted. Around 1970, Coby's father changed his view, as the household finances had improved somewhat.

Years later, after Coby married Arie van Baalen, a farmer's son, the couple decided to start their own two-pronged business in Brakel, Belgium: a dairy cattle farm and a dressage barn. Coby and Arie lived in a camper on their property for years because they could not obtain a permit to build a house. More than anything else, Coby and Arie wanted to start a family. Coby's desire to become a mother far surpassed her other desires. Marlies and Arie Junior were born. At that time, their parents could not have suspected that Arie would completely take after his father, and that Marlies would follow the example of her mother.

Coby found an enthusiastic supporter for her equestrian ambitions in her father-in-law, Arie van Baalen, Senior. Those ambitions would cost money, but one always has to spend money to make money. At that time, Coby turned down a high offer to purchase the up-and-coming horse Natrial, as she was hoping for an international dressage career with him. The dream did not come true with Natrial: he became ill. The dream was still not realized with the next talented horse, Biraldo. His owners sold him to another rider to compete in the Olympics. The third try was a charm, however. Coby fulfilled all her ambitions with her third horse, the black KWPN stallion, Olympic Ferro, owned by Jan Lamers and Adriaan van der Goor. Coby first saw the stallion when he was eight years old at her barn's breeding station and became immediately captivated by him. She did not rest until she, together with Johann Hinnemann, had reached the highest level with the stallion. The 1998 World Cup in Rome was their first big appearance, where they won the team silver medal and sixth place individually. Many successes followed, including placing second during the Dressage World Cup Finals in 's-Hertogenbosch in spring, 2000. At the Olympic Games in Sydney, they earned the team silver medal and placed fifth individually. Opportunity was all Coby needed to make her dreams come true.

Coby has motivated and inspired many students to reach Grand Prix level. This has even, on two occasions, resulted in an individual gold medal winner. In 1998, her daughter, Marlies, won the individual gold and team gold medals with the Dutch dressage team during the European Championships for Juniors in Hickstead. A year later, Belgian rider Delphine Meiresonne won the individual gold medal on her pony, Noble Casper, at the European Cup for Ponies.

The Simplicity of Dressage

Starting Points and the End Goal

Durchlässigkeit

Principles for Training

Chapter 1

The End Goal: Durchlässigkeit

"The Simplicity of Dressage. *The longer I think about it, the more I like the title of this book,"* *says Coby van Baalen. "I have always found riding far from simple, but little by little, the pieces of the puzzle seem to fit together. I still think good riding is difficult, but I understand it better all the time because the foundation of successful training for a jumper or a dressage horse always comes down to the same basic concepts."*

For years, Germans have based their riding theory on "the training scale." This scale is based on six main concepts that play a part during a horse's entire training. Every prominent trainer in Germany knows these concepts from memory and recognizes the relationship each one has with the other concepts.

German riding theory describes the term *durchlässigkeit* as something to strive for continuously and as the end goal of dressage schooling. *Durchlässigkeit* is difficult to translate; it translates roughly as "complete suppleness and continual total throughness of all the aids." In this book, Coby van Baalen and her trainer, Johann Hinnemann, strive to ensure that *durchlässigkeit* is the desired and achieved outcome of completing all six components of the dressage training scale.

Achieving *durchlässigkeit* is, therefore, the end goal of all training. The word may be difficult, but the meaning is simple: It is about the horse being free from tightness or stiffness; the horse does not resist anywhere in his muscles and always listens to the aids of the rider with obedience and suppleness. He "lets" the aids of the rider "through," resulting in *durchlässigkeit*. "You can only ride a horse well if he allows you to sit, gives you his back, and is on the aids," says van Baalen. "In other words, the horse reacts to the leg and gives nicely to the bit. He lets every aid you give come through and responds immediately. His movements swing through his whole body without any disturbances. If that is the case, then you are riding well! This can happen at every level, whether you ride Training Level on a young horse or Grand Prix on a more advanced horse."

arlies van Baalen riding idermark in piaffe, oerde, 2001.

You can only ride a horse well if he lets you sit correctly: Johann Hinnemann on Ideaal, Dortmund, 1988.

Systematic but Not Inflexible

Van Baalen has taken lessons from Hinnemann for more than ten years. His system is therefore hers, and Hinnemann's system is simply the German system. This well-organized method is described in the German National Equestrian Federation's (GNEF) study books used in Warendorf's instructor training program, including *Principles of Riding* and *Advanced Techniques of Dressage* (see Recommended Reading, p. 123), and upholds schooling a horse very systematically, which, according to van Baalen, "is different from inflexible and schematic. Every horse dictates the pace at which he trains and the order of his schooling, because every horse, naturally, has his peculiarities, his strengths and weaknesses, that have to be considered in his training."

Hinnemann agrees. "Everything is connected," he says. "You can talk about good or bad riding but not a well or poorly followed system."

Schooling

In this book, van Baalen and Hinnemann deal with several principles, one of which is "schooling" the horse. They prefer to use the term "schooling" rather than "training." "We don't talk about training a horse obedience, of course," van Baalen explains. "We discuss schooling a horse using gymnastics to physically and mentally develop him to the full potential of his natural abilities." International dressage rules state the following: The horse should be harmoniously developed "in his organic and natural qualities." As a result, the horse becomes "lively, obedient, and calm in his movement." This schooling of a horse is also called "systematic gymnasticizing."

Another principle upholds that a green, unschooled horse should be taught by an experienced rider. Inexperienced riders should learn to ride on experienced horses,

IDEAAL

(Doruto out of Karina by Eufraat), bred by P.L. Aarts in Heeswijk-Dinther, born in 1975.

Doruto is the unsurpassed producer of Grand Prix dressage horses in the Dutch breeding program to date. With the Doruto son, Ideaal, Hinnemann won the individual silver medal during the 1986 Dressage World Cup in Cedar Valley and the individual bronze medal during the 1987 Dressage European Cup at Goodwood. Ideaal is the prototype of a horse that is *durchlässig*, completely on the aids, after a long and successful training period. Hinnemann emphasizes that this ideal picture of *durchlässigkeit* can only be achieved with a horse that is exceptionally enthusiastic, willing, and devoted to his work.

"At the end of the day," says Hinneman, "the quality of the horse also determines whether you actually win medals—his movement, the quality of his passage and piaffe, his entire presence. However, the horse's temperament dictates whether you will achieve the perfect stage of *durchlässigkeit* without any blocks or resistance. Ideaal was always incredibly devoted to his rider. As a trainer, I found it fantastic to see that his subsequent riders, Sven and Gonnelien Rothenberger, could also ride beautiful tests on him. He wanted to perform for his rider and opened himself to that completely. In that respect, Ideaal was ideal."

Ideaal is the prototype of a horse that is durchlässig, completely on the aids, after a long and successful training period. His cooperative and willing temperament contributed significantly to his success.

Dutch National Coach Jürgen Koschel and his silver medal team in Sydney, 2000, with (left to right) Arjen Teeuwissen, Anky van Grunsven, Coby van Baalen, and Ellen Bontje.

"schoolmasters." "That sounds so logical," says van Baalen, "but there are still many parents who buy young, green ponies for their young, inexperienced children who are only just learning to ride. That is not an ideal learning situation for the child or the pony. In this book, we assume that experienced riders are schooling their horses or ponies."

The Six Concepts

The constant flow of the aids through the horse does not just happen for the rider. German riding theory describes three stages in schooling a horse. The first stage is the "habituation and familiarization phase." In this phase, a young, green horse learns to accept the rider's weight on his back and to find his balance with this additional weight.

Rhythm and *losgelassenheit* are key in this first phase. *Losgelassenheit* is a German word that is again difficult to translate but roughly means "letting loose," or in other words, "relaxation" or "suppleness." Hinnemann states, "*Losgelassenheit* is the key to every success in riding. The word used most often during my lessons is *locker*, which means 'loose.' Regardless of the exercise or transition, the first order of business is always looseness. That is the foundation of everything."

The second phase of schooling aims at stimulating the use of the hind legs and confirming the horizontal balance even more, as the horse has, at this point, achieved horizontal balance under the rider. During this period, an average of two years, contact and *schwung* become very significant. The word *schwung*, or "impulsion," connotes a swinging action that is active, forward, energetic, and loose.

The third phase of schooling a horse is the most difficult. In this phase, carrying power must be developed. The horse must shift his balance from a horizontal balance to a balance on the hindquarters. The words "straightness" and "collection" belong with this phase of schooling.

"I'm certain," says van Baalen, "that any prominent German jumping or dressage trainer can immediately name the six concepts: Rhythm, *losgelassenheit* or suppleness, contact, impulsion, straightness, and collection. These six concepts comprise the thread that connects the story in any German teaching video. Therefore, training and riding theory are also as clear. The desired foundation for every riding horse is clear in principle. It's actually simple. If you continually keep these concepts in mind, concepts that are all connected and constantly influence one another, then you should be successful in schooling your horse. Of course, one horse may be more talented than another; he has great rhythm, for example, while the rhythm of another horse will always need attention. However, that's also what makes riding so exciting. You're working with living material, and there's always something to learn."

FIDERMARK

(Sire: Florestan I out of Watonga by Werther), born in 1992, bred by Wilhelm Hage in Rüther, Germany. This approved stallion, property of the Nordrhein-Westfälisches Landgestüt, was the reserve champion at the Nordrhein Westfalen stallion inspection in 1994. Fidermark became Bundes Champion in 1996. In 2002, he had eleven approved sons, of which Feinsinn is the most well-known.

The chestnut stallion Fidermark stood out his entire life because of his incredible natural suppleness and ease. "He's like a rubber ball," says van Baalen. "Everything swings on him, and everything he does swings. Whether he trots a simple 20-meter circle like a First Level horse, or moves laterally in a half-pass, or collects himself for the piaffe, everything is correct with him. Every movement swings and flows through his entire body." Fidermark is nice and light to ride because of his natural suppleness.

"A real 'dream horse' and very well suited to a young rider such as Marlies van Baalen," says Hinnemann. "He is sensitive and has a temperament that is entirely geared towards people. Fidermark is really a horse that allows his rider to feel what it is like to finally achieve perfect *durchlässigkeit*, even at the beginning of his schooling."

A section of Johann Hinnemann's beautiful training facility in Voerde, Germany.

Coby van Baalen at work at Dressuurstal van Baalen in Brakel, Belgium.

General Application

The six training principles apply to a young horse just starting out as well as to an advanced horse that is being further developed and is systematically worked on a regular basis.

"These training principles," explains Hinneman, "rhythm, *losgelassenheit*, a nice contact, impulsion in the movement, straightness, and collection—always apply. First, they're not just for dressage horses but also for horses that jump or horses trained for endurance. Second, they apply both to young horses that still have to learn to work systematically and to more advanced horses, as these horses still need to practice and reconfirm the a-b-c's of rhythm, *losgelassenheit*, and contact in the warm-up phase before they can progress to other things, such as collection."

Question:

Sport Horse Management

I have heard that it is a good idea to add certain supplements to feed as a preventive measure, for instance, supplements that help a horse's muscles, tissues, and tendons, and those that help prevent injuries. I want to maintain my horse, not indulge him. Do you think this is excessive? Should you just start thinking about this if you ride Third Level (Advanced Medium in the UK) or higher? I now ride Second Level (Medium in the UK). I certainly do not want to spend money on products that do not benefit my horse or me. Can you give me some advice?

Coby's Answer:

Keep Things Simple

My husband, Arie van Baalen, and I both come from agricultural backgrounds. Arie does the feeding at home, feeding the cows as well as the horses. We don't feed anything special: hay or silage, a complete feed and oats, according to each horse's needs. We get the hay or silage ourselves to ensure it's good quality. Beyond that, we try to provide our horses a lot of exercise and the correct training. I must honestly say that our horses always look in top shape. Horses that come to us for training are often accompanied by all kinds of buckets and jars containing all sorts of supplements. Of course, we gladly feed these to the horses. After a couple of weeks, Arie usually asks the client if he can try feeding the horse his way. The funny thing is, most of the horses start looking much better.

This is my experience: Feed as healthily and simply as possible. A horse should do well with this, combined with plenty of exercise and good riding, although there are always exceptions.

Training

The first time I went to Johann Hinnemann's barn ten years ago, I immediately noticed that all the horses looked so fit, healthy, and shiny. Their coats were beautiful; just lovely. They didn't look that way because of pills and powders and feed supplements, preventive or otherwise. Do you know why they looked so good? They had correct training! If you ensure that your horses are always very supple, really supple through the body, constantly round with energy flowing over the back, swinging in the movement, then you'll have a healthy and fit horse that looks good. Good training is everything, combined with good quality feed.

If a problem arises, despite all your good training, then consult a specialist. That's what I do. Have your vet check your horse's blood. Upon your vet's recommendation, have a good physiotherapist, chiropractor, or acupuncturist check your horse's back and neck. Look at your horse's hooves critically to determine if they are skillfully shod and if your horse stands straight and on all four feet. I've noticed that fashions take hold in what I think is the ethically questionable side of alternative medicine. Sometimes all horses suddenly have a liver problem; then all at once they all have a something wrong with their kidneys. I cannot accept that almost all horses will suddenly have a similar problem. I do, however, think they are often trained incorrectly. They're ridden so that they become tight instead of loose. No powder will help that—only good lessons, much patience, and endless practice, based on regularity and rhythm. I wish you success!

HRH Prince Willem Alexander benefits from Coby van Baalen's extensive knowledge during the Olympic Games in Sydney, 2000.

LAURENTIANER

(Sire: Lauries Crusador xx out of Gardena B by Grande), born in 1994, bred by Heinz Katt in Stade, Germany. This approved stallion, property of the Nordrhein-Westfälisches Landgestüt, won the stallion performance test in 1997 and received an incredible score of 10 for his desire to work. In 2000, Laurentianer became world champion among the six-year-old horses at the World Cup in Arnhem.

The stamp of Laurentianer's Thoroughbred sire is evident in his easy, light movement. "He has incredible freedom of shoulder movement and can 'play' with his front legs. You need these qualities to give expression to the collected movements and to make an impression in the dressage arena," says Hinnemann.

Laurentianer's light movement allows him to be ridden very nicely on the aids, and he continually demonstrates that complete responsiveness to the aids can be achieved. "It's a big advantage to have a horse with both a conformation and a temperament that lends itself to training," says van Baalen.

Laurentianer and Marlies van Baalen as a successful team on the Light Tour, 2002.

Riders of many nationalities feel comfortable with Johann Hinnemann as mentor and trainer. From left to right: Canadian Leonie Bramall on Gilbona; Coby van Baalen on Bas; and American Kathleen Raine on Avontuur.

Chapter 2

Principles for Training

Here again are the six basic training principles to strive for: rhythm, losgelassenheit (suppleness and relaxation), contact, impulsion, straightness, and collection. These principles combined result in the maximum effectiveness of the rider's aids. The horse is durchlässig: He is fully prepared and able to accept the rider's aids, to understand them, and to respond with the desired action.

Harmony

The quality of the rider determines whether, after correct training, all the desired qualities for a riding horse will be developed to their fullest. In order to achieve this, a rider must be able to evaluate the horse's temperament and psyche thoroughly. Further, the rider needs to provide the horse with sufficiently varied work. Coby van Baalen explains, "Even the most enjoyable work can become boring if it never changes. Even children get tired of eating cookies and candy everyday."

The quality of the horse determines whether he can be successfully trained to Grand Prix level in all respects. "Grand Prix is very difficult for both horse and rider," says Johann Hinnemann. "It cannot be expected that every rider and every horse will attain it. I feel it's extremely important for a trainer to evaluate the natural performance limitations of every horse and rider. Riding is a sport of harmony, which means the rider must be able to keep rhythm and to be 'in tune' with the horse. To this end, a rider who trains with consistency and understanding will certainly achieve the stated goals. The 'oneness' of horse and rider is most important. Achieving a level of complete harmony with the horse should be the aim of every rider and every instructor."

Lessons focusing on the seat are essential for the development of an independent seat and independent application of the aids. The horse can only be expected to move in balance when the rider's seat is independent. (A young Marlies van Baalen rides without stirrups under her mother's watchful eye on the Rivaal daughter, Casablanca, owned by Inge Fokker.)

Training Principles

If you want to successfully school your horse according to the system described in this book, you should first fully understand several principles. Most importantly, training should always be systematic, logical, and proceed from easy to difficult, with consideration for individual strengths and weaknesses of both horse and rider.

First, let's discuss the benefits of using a system. Training a horse demands systematic progression. One piece builds upon another. "For example," explains van Baalen, "you first teach a horse to go forward from your two legs. As soon as a horse understands that he must go forward from two legs, then you can teach him to move laterally from one leg. Then you can do a step of leg-yield. If he understands that, then you can go on and ask for a bit of shoulder-fore, and then some shoulder-in."

Another training principle stems from the preceding one: The training must progress logically, from easy to difficult. In this way, the rider develops the horse's physical condition and motor skills to perform the work. Hinnemann adds another example: "You first confirm a horse's balance and obedience with a lot of walk-trot transitions and trot-canter transitions. When those are perfect, then you try walk-canter transitions."

Back to the Basics

The principle of progressing from easy to difficult work requires that a rider always go back to basics when problems arise. The rider should return to work that the horse performs effortlessly. "It doesn't make any sense to keep repeating an exercise that's not going well in the hope that it eventually will," says van Baalen. "As a rule, things only get worse that way." In particular, with flying changes, many riders try endlessly to get a change without stopping to ask themselves if the horse possesses the basics necessary to do one.

Logical, systematic, progressing from easy to difficult, with understanding for individual strengths and weaknesses: These are the principles for successful training. This "golden" dream team undoubtedly knows all about them! From left to right: Laurens van Lieren, Marlies van Baalen, chef d'equipe Mara de Bel, Annemiek van der Vorm, and Joyce Heuitink. This team wrote history by winning the team gold medal in 2000 as well as 2001 at the European Dressage Championship for Young Riders (ages 21 and under).

"That happens extremely often," claims van Baalen. "It's incredible how many riders, who aren't my students, have nothing but tension and problems in the canter because they're working on changes. Changes never work when the canter is tense and has rhythm problems."

"The case may be," Hinnemann says, "that the horse needs to return to canter-walk-canter transitions for a while to get him properly on the driving and restraining aids and to make him straight again. After a period, if you have obedience and self-carriage in the canter and responsive hindquarters, then you can attempt a change again."

Specific Talent

Our modern warmblood breeders are more consistent than ever in breeding horses that are extremely suited to the work we ask of them. As van Baalen says, "An energetic horse with 'electric hind legs'—that's what we're all looking for to go to the top—but naturally, such a hot temperament is a bit difficult. You have to learn how to deal with it."

Not every horse is talented in all respects like Mielona. Coby van Baalen rode the Ster mare (sire: Millers Grey) to Third Level (Advanced Medium in the UK) dressage as well as jumping, 1976.

Not every horse is talented in all respects. Therefore, another basic training principle of a skilled rider is that he or she considers the individual talents of his or her horse.

Limits

Not every horse is inherently gifted enough to do well at Grand Prix. Every horse has his performance limits: physical, mental, or both. "Take a horse that stiffens his back after a few strides of extended trot and stops the movement from swinging through," says Hinnemann. "The extended trot is clearly too difficult for the horse. One of the previously stated basic principles says to return to work that is easier for the horse. Endless repetition only makes a horse unnecessarily tired, perhaps more unwilling, and causes him to make even more rhythm mistakes. In this case with this type of horse, you'd do a lot of tempo changes in the trot throughout the arena, continually coming back and then lengthening again, though not yet across the entire diagonal. For this purpose, the rider can help the horse by rising in the trot. At a certain point, the rider will feel the horse willingly respond to a request to lengthen for a few strides. The rider should take pleasure in that: a performance limitation was overcome. After several months, that horse may be strong enough to extend across the whole diagonal, and perhaps in the course of schooling, it will be evident that this was not a real limitation."

When training her horse, a skilled rider considers his unique talents. Riding Grand Prix requires great effort from both rider and horse; not everyone can expect to reach this level. Coby van Baalen is pictured here riding a half-pass on Olympic Ferro.

Consistency

Patience, self-control, and feeling are good qualities—especially for a rider. A rider with these qualities cannot err in the basic principle of training with consistency. "Being consistent sounds very logical, doesn't it?" says van Baalen. "If you think something is good today, then you also think it's good tomorrow. However, this is often not the case. Take the simple example of going to a show. How often do you see riders sitting on their horses, not concentrating on them at all? They walk their horses around, talking with others about this and that, and suddenly, it's time to seriously warm up. This type of rider evidently assumes that the horse immediately knows that it's time to be serious. Suddenly, the horse is attacked by the rider's aids, while just a minute ago, he was allowed to do whatever he wanted. This is not consistency, of course, and it's not fair to the horse." Van Baalen notices another example of inconsistent behavior in the halt. Riders often practice the halt when first schooling the horse: They have the horse nicely immobile; square; with good contact; and waiting for the rider. "However," says van Baalen, "later they get so busy with everything, halting correctly tends to fall by the wayside. What happens then? You want to go to a show, so you practice your test and the horse immediately gets a kick and a pull to let him know that he must immediately and correctly halt. You let weeks go by without any thought to the halt, and then that happens. Of course, that's not consistency. The horse doesn't deserve that. I must honestly say that I only learned to spend time on the halt everyday with Johann. There's a well-known German maxim that says a rider who doesn't get an 8 for his entry and halt only has

NATRIAL

(First Trial out of Itharin by Eufraat), breeder unknown, born in 1972.

"Natrial was really at a disadvantage because he was my first horse," says van Baalen. "I still needed to learn everything and practice endlessly before I had things mastered. I found it all so terribly difficult! It began with the flying changes. Finally, I became NVDR Light Tour Champion with Natrial. He was schooling all the Grand Prix movements when an injury, unfortunately, forced me to retire him."

Natrial is a good example because of what was accomplished despite his rider's limitations at that time and his own limitations. He was already nine years old when van Baalen got him, and he was small: only about 15.3 hands (159 cm). However, his small size didn't matter at all when he trotted "uphill" with his swinging movement. Then he was just impressive.

Natrial and Coby van Baalen during the KNF Championship, at Levade, 1983. The pair was third at Third Level (Advanced Medium in the UK) dressage. In 1984, they won the KNF Indoor Championship at Third Level, after which Natrial moved up from the lower levels to Grand Prix.

FESTIVO

(Sire: Frühlingsball by Prinzessin by Pasteur xx), born in 1985, comes out of a line of stallions that has brought the Rheinland much success. Festivo was one of the first stallions of the Nordrhein-Westfälisches Landgestüt for which a career was planned as a breeding stallion as well as a competitive dressage horse. He is not, at this time, used as a breeding stallion.

Van Baalen acquired Festivo to ride when he was twelve years old. It didn't take long before she showed him successfully on the Light Tour, thanks to his good temperament, natural impulsion, and wonderful rideability. "*Gehfreude*," says Hinnemann. "He exudes a general state of happiness when he works."

Young rider Danielle van Aalderen has a real schoolmaster with Festivo. "Every ambitious young rider should really have the chance to practice developing feel and their riding skills on such a schoolmaster," stresses van Baalen. "What's nice about this stallion is that he's always a reflection of how well Danielle rides. If Danielle rides average, then he goes average. If Danielle rides well, then he goes well. And if she rides super, he goes super!" In 2002, Danielle van Aalderen, a rider the same age as her horse, rode the former national stallion in her third European Championship

Festivo as Westfalen National Stallion, ridden by champion rider Klaus Tonsfeuerborn, Aachen, 1998.

Festivo with Coby van Baalen, winners of a Kür for breeding stallions showing at Fourth Level (Advanced Level in the UK), Essen, 1999.

A new career for Festivo with Danielle van Aalderen, 2000.

Riders often forget to practice the halt. Learn young, learn right. Arie van Baalen, Junior, on Gaston, and Marlies van Baalen on Anjonette, 1990.

himself to blame: He's not diligent and hasn't practiced enough. Of course, I hear that often. Apart from the scores at a show, practicing the halt is just a good exercise. It helps a young horse learn obedience and can be used as an exercise with an older horse to check if he is really on the aids and to bring his hind legs under his body."

Horsemanship

Finally, correct and successful horse training requires varied work. A horse must be content in his work. He won't remain content, however, riding mind-numbing identical circles everyday, and practicing and repeating exercises in exactly the same order. Riding is also called "the art of riding." Those who keep the basic horse training principles in mind come very close to practicing this art.

The following chapter deals with the first concept that consistently plays a major part in training every riding horse: Rhythm.

Question:

Horse Behavior

I have an eight-year-old gelding that was gelded when he was four. He was turned out in a pasture with mares and stallions as a three- and four-year-old. He's a very playful horse that has actually never grown up. I got him as a six-year-old. He jumped at Level 4 (Foxhunter in the UK) but had no experience in dressage. We have, however, in the past two years, quickly advanced from Training Level (Novice Level in the UK) to Second Level (Medium Level in the UK). You may think that things sound good so far.

Here's the problem: My horse is extremely attached to my sister's pony, a mare. The mare doesn't have any problem leaving my horse, but my horse has problems leaving the mare—especially at shows! Then, he'll buck. We thought he just felt good and would eventually settle down, but he just keeps getting worse. If the mare stays at home, then nine out of ten times, my ride goes well. However, if she comes along and he can't see her, he starts acting up. Tension builds until he finally explodes and starts bucking wildly. I'm no longer in the ribbons with him. How can I address this problem?

Coby's Answer:

Natural Horse Behavior

I'm very pleased with your question because it gives me the opportunity to explain something about natural and unnatural horse behavior.

By nature, horses live in herds with a leader. When you put a horse in a stall, you've identified yourself as his leader. You are the boss, but that doesn't mean that a horse's natural herd instinct disappears. If you ride in a group on the trail, the whole group always crosses over to another trail at the same time. And if your horse doesn't want to cross a "scary" bridge, then another herd member can often be helpful in taking the lead, as horses don't want to be left behind.

Your horse has a very strongly developed herd and leader instinct because he was a stallion for so long. Nevertheless, he needs to know that there's now a stronger leader: you. And he needs to listen to you. Often, horses that haven't been away from home display behavior similar to your horse. They stick with a known and trusted horse, usually a stablemate. One thing you can do is take your horse to a lot of new and different places, and accept that it'll be a long time before he concentrates on you as the rider in a strange place.

Now, for your horse. As long as your horse acts like this, you just have to be practical when you go to important shows: travel without the pony. In the long run, however, it's better to overcome this behavior. You need to be a more dominant leader with your horse than you already are. Be the boss. Be consistent. This begins with tying, grooming, and tacking up. Demand obedience. He has to stand still while you saddle him, for example. He also has to stand still while you mount. If he doesn't have any respect for you on the ground, you can't expect him to respect you when you ride him or when you're at a show.

I don't know how he bucks at a show or if he immediately gets you off his back. In any case, this is pure resistance and disobedience and is absolutely not allowed, not even out of exuberance. He has learned a bad habit, and he needs unlearn it as soon as possible. Everyday when you ride your horse at home, have someone lead the mare away and make your horse concentrate and pay attention to you. Let the pony come back, and then send her away again. Repeat this as long as your horse is concentrating on you. Punish him if you feel him tensing up: put him to work; ride him forward; canter him, for example, in smaller circles and do lots of trot-canter transitions, a few strides of lateral work, another transition; do the same on the other rein, and so on. It doesn't matter what happens, as long as you keep him working. If you feel him submit, then reward him extensively with your voice and let him chew the reins out of your hands. Only then can you begin to restore the desired pecking order between the two of you. You can't punish a horse for displaying natural behavior. You can, however, make use of it. That's exactly what every rider must do.

Spending time with a pony—letting him graze, brushing him, picking his feet—in short, doing a bit of everything, is initially more important for would-be riders than actually riding. That time spent caring for the pony develops a foundation of trust that is essential later for riding. Pictured: Marlies and Arie, July, 1989.

Question:

A Green Pony

My sister has a new pony. He's five years old and is a gelding. He's only newly saddle broke and still needs to learn everything else, even to be groomed.

A water bucket hangs in his stall. Once, my sister was grooming the pony, and he pinned her between the water bucket and himself!

The pony can be ridden nicely tracking left at the walk and trot, but at the canter, he jumps out of the arena. Tracking right, the walk and the trot are also good but not as good as to the left, and the pony also jumps out of the arena when cantering.

What can my sister do to get along with her new pony?

Coby's Answer:

About Being Green and Acquiring Experience

A new pony! That is, of course, a big experience in your life, and naturally, you are extremely happy. I know exactly how it is: I still have vivid memories of when I used to ride ponies. I spent entire Saturdays with a group of Pony Clubbers, wandering through the woods, a pack strapped to my back containing bread and a drink. We just talked and enjoyed our ponies. I sometimes remember that time with a pang of jealousy. If I only had time now for such carefree fun...when it's all about just enjoying your pony.

Not a Lap Dog

Your sister will only begin to enjoy her new pony if she is completely safe and can trust him. Children who are just developing an interest in horses often aren't that interested in riding but rather in playing, brushing, letting their ponies graze; in short, just being around them is the most important thing. A foundation of trust that is essential for riding stems from that "playing around." Unfortunately, as I read your letter, I don't see any foundation for this trust. First, I'd like to compliment you on your letter. As a concerned sister, you've recognized a problem between the new pony and your inexperienced sister, and you're seeking help. That's very wise, and therefore, I'm very pleased with your question.

However, reading your letter really shocked me: A pony that has already pinned your sister in his stall between the water bucket and himself! Fortunately, the incident apparently ended well, but it could have turned out differently. Ponies and horses are many times stronger than we are. However sweet and easy they sometimes become over time, they never become "lap dogs." In theory, they remain dangerous animals with which you shouldn't take any risks. I always promptly discourage parents from buying green ponies for their inexperienced children. A pony may be very beautiful, but why go looking for problems? In theory, an inexperienced child belongs on a very trustworthy, super-experienced pony. Then you can learn how to ride and to sit relaxed, the foundation for giving good aids.

Stallions

I also frequently see girls get a little experience riding dressage and then think they need to buy a stallion. Some parents, too, are afraid of a mouse, so to speak, but they insist on buying a stallion. Why is this necessary? People say a stallion has more presence, but a stallion involves risks, certainly at shows. Why should one deliberately and consciously go looking for problems?

I definitely know what I'm talking about because I've ridden many stallions in the past and continue to do so. My daughter, Marlies, also rode a pony stallion, Dancer, but only after she had won three basic championships, and that stallion had already been successful at FEI level with his previous rider in Germany. Furthermore, I never let Marlies ride Dancer alone. She was professionally instructed, which is also necessary. If we went to a show, the pony was first ridden or longed at home. At shows, he was also usually longed before Marlies got on him. A child can never judge the power of a fresh pony, let alone the power of a pony whose stallion tendencies suddenly let loose.

Riding remains a sport with risks. However, you can certainly try to reduce those risks as much as possible. That's what I always try to do, even now. At a show, I've even climbed on our stallion, Inspekteur, in my high heels and dress pants just before the ribbons were awarded! Marlies was eighteen years old at that time and very gutsy, and Inspekteur is very obedient, but he's a breeding stallion during the summer season, and I could see that the summer sun had focused his mind completely on breeding. I therefore got on him and really cantered him forward to get his concentration back on his rider again. Horses aren't robots.

Take Care of Number One

I realize the above tirade about green children riding experienced ponies doesn't really help you because you already have your pony. You need to make the best of the situation. I certainly hope, however, that the above warning has discouraged all parents in the future from buying a green pony for their inexperienced child.

Back to Your Pony

Make training the pony, ensuring safety, and avoiding risks priority number one. That means your sister should always have help. Be clear and consistent in all that you do. Groom the pony in cross-ties to prevent him from spinning around and pinning anyone. Longe him often. Let an experienced rider teach the pony manners under saddle and that jumping out of the arena is forbidden. Take him to an indoor a few times so that you can ride him without him jumping out of the arena. Don't let your sister back on the pony until he has learned to be more obedient. This is the only advice I can give, and while I know it won't be fun, it will be worth it to prevent your sister from having a possible accident with her pony. I wish you much success and wisdom. Finally, I wish you safe enjoyment with your pony.

Naomi, the miniature horse, with Debora Pijpers and her mother.

MIDGRAAF'S ANJONETTE

(Sire: Bengad Cockles), **born in 1978**

Trustworthy ponies are worth their weight in gold. Some ponies are ridden by three or four different riders, year after year, at the European Championships. Anjonette was Stal van Baalen's first family pony. She came to the barn when Marlies was four years old. The pony was fine in her stall, but feeding her grain made her too strong under saddle for Marlies. "Marlies took lessons on school horses for a year to restore her confidence. A more experienced girl rode Anjonette during that time," explains van Baalen. When Marlies was six years old, she began her career on Anjonette.

"We quickly had to promise Marlies and Arie Junior that we'd never sell Anjonette," van Baalen goes on. "We've kept our promise. We've never sold her, but we always let new kids borrow her. Her present rider has renamed her 'Habibi' in honor of our Marlies' horse, the 1998 European Champion."

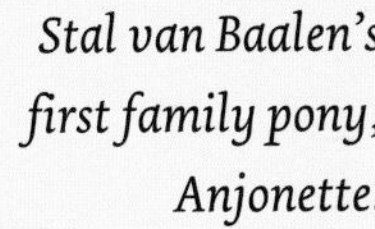

Stal van Baalen's first family pony, Anjonette.

The Habituation

and Familiarization Phase

Rhythm

Losgelassenheit

Chapter 3

Rhythm

Rhythm is the first reoccurring basic concept in schooling dressage. A horse has three basic gaits— the walk, the trot, and the canter—and each basic gait has its own rhythm. Rhythm means the pure beat of the movement. The walk is a striding and suspensionless gait; the trot and canter are both motions with impulsion and suspension. A pure rhythm is extremely important when schooling a horse and must never be lost—not with a young horse, not with a more advanced horse, not when introducing something new in training, never. The rider must maintain rhythm at all times.

"If a horse ever starts making rhythm mistakes and moving unevenly," says Johann Hinnemann, "the rider should immediately return to easier work so that the horse can find his rhythm again. Rhythm is the foundation of movement and never should be compromised—not for one second."

The Walk

The walk is a striding, four-beat movement: The horse picks up and sets down each foot independently of the others. This action occurs in eight phases. Sometimes two feet are on the ground; other times three feet are on the ground. "Identifying the successive walk rhythm seems complicated," says Coby van Baalen. "However, practice makes perfect. Riders can develop a feel for the walk most efficiently through observation and practice in the saddle."

The structure of the walk is an alternating tripedal-diagonal-tripedal-lateral movement (right front, left hind, left front, right hind). A distinct four-beat rhythm can be heard clearly on hard ground. If you look at the front and hind leg on one side, you should see the legs forming a "V" from the side at a certain point: When the hind leg moves forward, it should drive the front leg forward, so to speak, almost touching it.

Iarlies van Baalen on
Iabibi, Arnhem, 1998.

A young horse just started under saddle should learn to walk quietly and to become accustomed to the rider's driving aids. In the early stages of a horse's training, the rider should only take a light feel of the reins in the walk; otherwise, rhythm mistakes and unevenness will quickly arise. "The rider needs to follow the horse's natural nodding motion of his neck and his body in the walk with relaxed elbows, wrists, and shoulders," says Hinnemann.

This six-year-old, approved, Westfalian pony stallion Top Yellow (sire: Till the Champ) ridden by the European Pony Champion, Delphine Meiresonne, has received a 9 for his walk numerous times. "A rider can ruin even this naturally outstanding walk if she's not careful to let the movement go through the body!" warns van Baalen. Top Yellow demonstrates the extended walk...

...and the collected walk. Notice the difference in the head and neck position.

HABIBI

(Ulft x Wendelien *keur*/sport/preferred/performance by Onyx), bred by Marjan Dorresteijn, born in 1989. Half-sister, Finesse, out of the same dam, is also profiled in this book.

Marlies van Baalen's champion horse, Habibi, is a shining example of a horse with excellent rhythm. He always keeps his rhythm effortlessly, whether he moves laterally or straight ahead; whether he walks, trots or canters; and whether he lengthens or shortens.

"Judges always write compliments on his protocols about his excellent rhythm," says van Baalen. "He was complimented on his rhythm in Hickstead in 1998 when he became the European Champion. He even displays this ability in the collected walk and the extended walk. I don't know many horses that can naturally do that so easily and well. Habibi really has natural talent."

Habibi is a horse that naturally has very rhythmical movement.

DANCER

(Dandy x Valentino), born in 1983.

Marlies van Baalen acquired Dancer when Johann and Gisela Hinneman's daughter, Bettina, outgrew the pony stallion. Says van Baalen, "I think it's very important for young children to have the opportunity to develop feel on a nice pony. Dancer has helped Marlies develop a lot of feel. At first, she thought that big stallion neck in front of her was very scary. She really had to get used to it!"

Dancer was almost picture perfect but had one difficulty: His trot would sometimes get hurried. Then he would lose his rhythm a bit. "As a result of that problem, Marlies has developed a lot of feel for rhythm and self-carriage," van Baalen continues. "She also got her first experience with straightness on Dancer and discovered that she had to canter him energetically forward at a show. Otherwise, he could become too much of a stallion in the arena. She kept him focused on his work by cantering him forward. In short, she learned a lot from him."

Marlies van Baalen won her first international medal in 1993 with Dancer. Pictured next to Dancer is their coach, Jo Willems.

Marlies eventually rode Dancer in the European Championships for Ponies in both 1993 and 1994 in Hasselt, Belgium, and won the team silver medal.

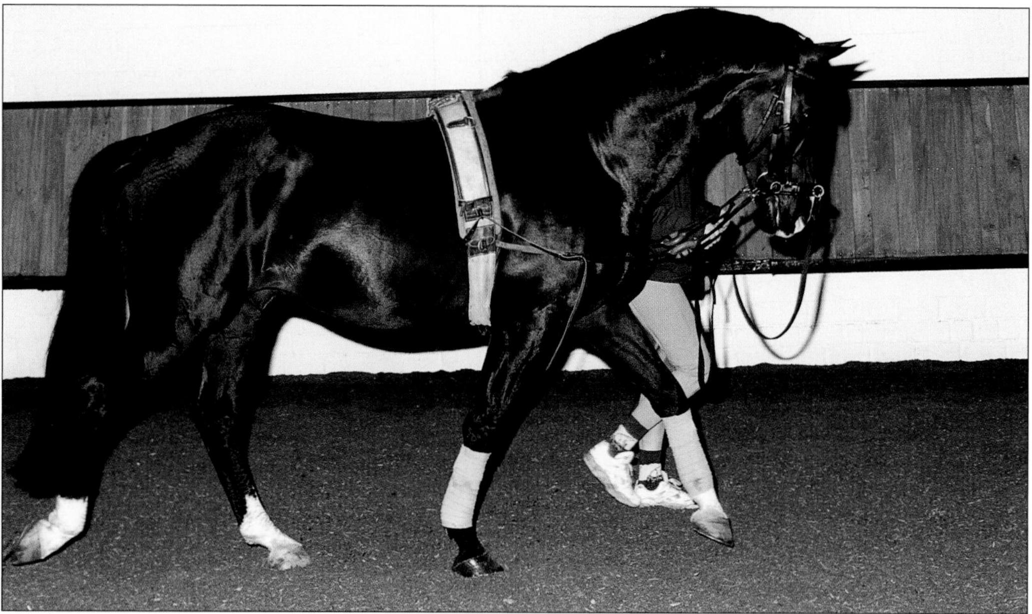

A correct walk can also be maintained by walking with a relaxed back in correctly fitted side reins, as Olympic Ferro demonstrates here. Notice the light cavesson and how the side reins are fastened. Putting them around the surcingle and through the rings helps keep the horse between the reins.

A rider should absolutely never force a certain headset with the hands. In the walk, this can be disastrous. Once an impure walk is confirmed—such as the pace, in which the horse moves his front and hind legs forward together on the same side—it is difficult to correct.

Another common rhythm mistake in the walk is "the short-long walk" when one hind leg or front leg takes a longer stride than the other. This mistake is also caused by excessive backward use of the hand.

According to Hinnemann, a young horse just started under saddle needs to get used to training sessions and therefore should be walked quietly on a long rein for ten to fifteen minutes prior to beginning the day's lesson. "That was an adjustment for me!" van Baalen exclaims. "I always used to be in a rush, so I would begin trotting right away. Furthermore, I rode for a lot of stallion owners, and they like to see some action and show—a spectacular trot, for instance. When I started training with Johann, I had to entirely unlearn all of that. I then discovered I was better off riding fewer horses everyday but riding them quietly and well, than I was riding any number of horses in a hurried fashion."

"If a young horse is too fresh to ride quietly at the walk," Hinneman says, "you need to ask yourself if he's getting too much protein or not enough exercise during the rest of the day. Perhaps the horse needs exercise on the walker, in hand, on the longe-line, in the paddock, or in the pasture. I think walking under saddle at the beginning of a training session is very important. Walking ensures that the joints, muscles, and tendons have a chance to gradually warm-up. It also maintains the walk as the walk, one of the three basic gaits. It confirms certain obedience from the horse and is good for establishing psychological relaxation and calmness. Finally, it gives horse and rider an opportunity to focus and connect with one another."

Delphine Meiresonne again, this time with Noble Casper. Medium walk.

An extended walk.

"I'm certainly not the only one who didn't used to take the time to walk," van Baalen states. "In general, the walk isn't practiced enough during training. People often think it's boring. Don't forget that the walk has a coefficient of 2 in upper level tests. It's definitely worth practicing for a score that is worth double. Furthermore, a score is given at the bottom of every protocol at every level for the purity of the gaits. That score will never be high if the walk—one of the three basic gaits—isn't correct."

The Trot

The trot is a swinging, two-beat movement with four different phases. The horse alternates the moment of suspension in turns by putting down and picking up again the

Three of photos of the KWPN stallion Inspekteur.

Pictured standing.

As a three-year-old ridden by Merieke Voorneveld during the stallion performance testing.

Inspekteur as an eight-year-old captured in exactly the same movement as above. His muscle development and expressive, rhythmic movement are clearly evident.

one diagonal pair (left hind and right front) and then the other (right hind and left front).

A young horse should be ridden nicely forward on straight and curved lines, without chasing the horse beyond his natural tempo. A horse should first learn to trot securely balanced and relaxed under the rider's weight. Rising at the trot will reduce stress to the horse's back muscles. The trot is the easiest gait for the horse to seek contact with the rider's hand. A nice, rhythmic trot produces consistently clean movement and equal, rhythmic strides. "Rhythm must be maintained on straight lines, curved lines,

BIRALDO

(Sire: Rinaldo out of Pexilia, sire: Exilio xx), bred by: J.A. de Breuk, born in 1983, was the first horse that Coby van Baalen rode to Grand Prix. Biraldo ultimately took part in the 1992 Olympic Games, where he placed a commendable 12th with Canadian Chistilot Boylen-Hansen.

As a four-year-old, Biraldo was already the Dutch champion riding horse with the best gaits because of his outstanding rhythm and length of stride. He had exceptionally expressive movement. He also had disadvantages. He was somewhat overbuilt and had a less than ideal neck, which always made contact difficult. "Biraldo's naturally pure rhythm was precisely the reason why he could, to a certain extent, do all the Grand Prix movements as a six-year-old. However, I still wasn't very experienced," says van Baalen.

In 1989, Biraldo was the first horse van Baalen took to Hinnemann for lessons and advice. She has been with him ever since. "I remember I had trouble in the passage with Biraldo," van Baalen explains. "Johann wanted to see me do all the movements. He also got on Biraldo. Then he started passaging right away, assuming there wouldn't be any problem. When I saw that easy, natural way of riding, I thought I really needed to keep my eyes and ears open. I could really learn something here! That was right. I continue to learn—at home and with Johann Hinnemann. There's always something to learn with horses."

Biraldo is a horse with a great deal of expression in his rhythm and movement. He is pictured here in piaffe, 1991.

POWER AND PAINT

(Sire: Power Boy out of Golden Dream, sire: Dancer), born in 1993. Power and Paint, whose grand sire is the pony stallion Dancer, was reserve champion at the stallion *Keuring* in 1995. He later participated in the stallion performance testing in 1998, which he won. In 2002, Marrigje van Baalen rode in her first International Pony European Championship with the stallion and won the team silver medal.

"You can't expect young children who need to learn how to ride their tests well to also know how to solve big training problems they may have with their ponies. That's why you should always try to start with a pony that has three correct basic gaits and a pure rhythm," says van Baalen. Her niece, Marrigje van Baalen, first rode Devito, a pony who could trot and canter spectacularly, but his walk was a problem: He tended to pace. "We learned right away that three correct gaits are by far preferable to two spectacular and one problematic gait," explains van Baalen. "There's no advantage to an incredible, 'to-die-for' trot if another gait is lacking. Marrigje couldn't correct the pacing in the tests. Power and Paint allowed her to feel three correct basic gaits."

Power and Paint has three very rhythmic, correct gaits.

in turns, and in transitions," says Hinneman. "No exercise or transition can be good if rhythm mistakes are connected with it. Any advancement in the horse's training can't be good if it leads to rhythm mistakes."

The rider's calves must always lie quietly on the horse's sides without constantly driving or taking the leg completely off. "You have to keep your lower leg on a horse that runs from the aids," explains van Baalen, "otherwise, he'll never grow accustomed to the leg and will only become more unsure, nervous, and overly sensitive to the leg aids. You'll never make a nervous horse quiet by keeping your leg off of him but rather by keeping your leg on him. By the same token, if a lazy horse is driven too much by a constantly banging leg, he'll become dulled and desensitized to the driving aids."

Rhythm mistakes in the trot appear as a slight unevenness or slight lameness without obvious physical cause. "Rhythm mistakes can also be seen in the slow, passage-like trot, which many Third Level (Advanced Medium Level in the UK) riders unfortunately think is great," points out van Baalen. "Such horses are often not completely in front of the leg and often keep one front leg still in the air longer than the other. In contrast, a collected horse doing a real passage is characterized by faster and more rhythmic movement rather than slow and uneven. The remedy is always to ride forward with the seat and both legs and regain the rhythm."

The Canter

The canter is a swinging, powerful, three-beat movement with six different phases. A horse can canter on the left lead and on the right lead, which is termed after the leg that reaches farthest forward. After the moment of suspension, the horse lands on his outside hind leg. Then the horse puts his inside hind and outside front diagonal leg pair on the ground. Then he lifts his outside hind while the diagonal pair remain on the ground, followed by the placement of his inside front leg on the ground, the consequent lifting of the diagonal pair, and finally the horse picks up his front leg. This is followed by the moment of suspension (see the photo series in Chapter Nine).

"If you watch a cantering horse, the canter has to immediately look easy," says van Baalen. "It just has to be naturally pleasing. The canter shouldn't look slow, as though the horse can fall out of the canter at any moment; it shouldn't look hurried either, preventing the horse from nicely completing his stride."

Adds Hinnemann, "You shouldn't severely punish a horse for a wrong canter depart. This only leads to tension and constriction, which results in another wrong depart. An incorrect canter depart results from difficulties with balance. A rider should therefore return to a quiet trot tempo and then try again. The rider can help the horse by finding a good departure spot in the arena, for example, on the circle as he approaches the rail."

If you watch a cantering horse, the canter must immediately look easy. Coby van Baalen on Olympic Ferro, Aachen, 1998.

The canter must be a clear jump. If the horse understands the canter, then the rider can add some simple tempo changes to the work. "The rider encourages the horse's hind leg to move under his body more actively in the canter by driving more with the legs," explains van Baalen. "At first, the rider can only half-halt occasionally to a slower tempo because the horse hasn't yet learned to keep his balance under the rider in a slow tempo. Shortening the tempo means that the hind legs have to be more active and move more quickly. However, you often see a broken canter—a four-beat canter—with horses that are kept at a slow tempo but aren't completely activated behind to move under themselves more. In those cases, I strongly recommend practice lengthening and shortening the stride. Reward the horse when he understands your intentions; that can't be done too much or too often."

More About Rhythm Mistakes

A rider needs to take the time in his education to understand and develop feel for the horse's gaits. "Some riders naturally have a lot of feel for a particular gait," says van Baalen. "You see some riders who always ride their horses at the trot with good swing and energy but who usually don't do well in the canter. Of course, the opposite is true as well. As a rider, it's important to take the time to develop feel in all the gaits. Only then can you learn to develop the horse's gaits themselves."

It takes an average of one and a half years to provide a horse with a solid basic training foundation. This basic training includes confirming rhythm in all three gaits as well as developing *losgelassenheit* (complete suppleness and relaxation), contact, and impulsion. "There are horses that require more time because their muscles take longer to develop or their mental development demands they be allowed more breaks in their work," amends Hinnemann. "As soon as a horse starts making rhythm mistakes or displaying tension, he should go back to an earlier stage

The two European Junior Championship horses canter together in a joyful victory lap: Habibi ridden by Marlies van Baalen and Noble Casper ridden by Delphine Meiresonne. Both horses really push off the ground and clearly canter "uphill." Coincidentally, both horses are just in the canter phase in which they've landed on the outside hind leg after the suspension moment. Next, they will place their inside diagonals on the ground.

in his work; a stage that was easy for the horse. That sounds like a time-consuming affair, but going back is actually always the shortest way. Returning to the basics is the only road that leads to improvement and subsequently successful progress in schooling." Hinnemann continues, gladly providing a practical example: the counter-canter. "If the horse is much too fast in the counter-canter or loses rhythm in a slower canter, then the horse has a problem with his balance. The remedy for this is to do a lot of tempo changes on a circle by repeatedly riding forward to a medium canter and then returning to the working canter, until the horse really carries himself when asked to shorten his stride. Then you can try a bit of counter-canter again."

Rhythm mistakes usually arise when a rider uses too much hand and too little driving leg, which, in contrast, would invite the horse to relax his back and come through in his movements. The hand is always a disrupting force in the horse's balance. If a rider uses too much pressure on one rein, the horse can even appear "rein lame" through rhythm mistakes. "Ride the horse really forward for a few days and let him chew the reins out of your hands multiple times," advises van Baalen. "Ride the horse long and low, and then bring him up again."

Rhythm mistakes are often connected with problems with the contact, tension mistakes, or a tight back. Sometimes a horse resists without a clear cause; perhaps the horse is not completely healthy or is pushed too hard. Says Hinnemann, "The horse always determines the pace of the training; therefore, problems must always be taken seriously. There's no sense in using different bits or auxiliary reins. These appear to be solutions, but they treat the symptoms of a problem rather than the problem itself. A thoughtful rider looks for the root of the problem and begins working on it from there."

Question:

A "Passagey" Trot

My horse is seven years old, and I believe he's quite talented. I show at Second Level (Medium Level in the UK) and usually have good scores. I must admit, however, that I don't really understand what is meant by a "passagey" trot. I know it isn't good, but doesn't it concern horses that trot over the ground with more elevation? I don't understand why such a "passagey" trot is not accepted. Aren't a beautiful extended trot and an ordinary lengthened trot both good? I've discussed this with a few other riders, and they feel the same as I do. Perhaps you can clarify this for us.

Coby's Answer:

The "Passagey" Trot

Thanks for your question! A beautiful, lengthened trot is certainly good because it improves the horse's natural gaits. A trot that only emphasizes elevation is incorrect, as it doesn't include technically correct collection. A horse with a "passagey" trot won't do correct small circles and will only do a half-pass in a kind of extended trot, because this kind of horse won't bend at all. He doesn't bring his hind legs sufficiently under his center of gravity. Furthermore, he lifts his legs too high and doesn't move them forward enough.

I can certainly see how misunderstandings arise about this, however. In the past, when I used to present a number of stallions at shows for their owners, I rode quite differently than I do now. At that time, I rode the horses with as much elevation in the trot as possible, and I did a lot of extended trot. I didn't think it was bad if they were a bit tense or tight over the topline because that gave them more front leg action, which the breeders enjoyed seeing the most. That's what I thought at the time. I now know that today's breeders value correct training and show results more than pure circus tricks.

I must honestly say that this method of encouraging a tight back and tense front legs that extend like daisy cutters has no training or gymnasticizing value. Tempo changes are only good when a horse moves from his hindquarters, and that movement goes through his body and swings in the same rhythm. Bringing the tempo back again also has to take place from the hindquarters while maintaining rhythmic, even strides. This has to happen without the horse tightening his back and coming against the hand.

When I talk about an undesirable passagey trot, I'm talking about a trot in which the horse slows his rhythm. At first glance, the horse may appear to have an impressive, elevated trot; however, the horse has greatly slowed his tempo and rhythm at the same time, while the goal of dressage schooling is to make the horse's hindquarters move more quickly. The rider motivates the horse to bend the joints in his hindquarters more and to bring his hindquarters further under his mass. The opposite occurs with a passagey trot. The hindquarters slow rather than quicken. You might even think for a moment that the horse is passaging, but you'll find that the horse can't piaffe from that trot because the movement of the hindquarters is too big and too slow.

A rider can't work with a passagey trot. Once established, changing this trot is usually difficult, and the horse is often slow in his responses. If you always have to ride in a really quick tempo, can't bend your horse properly around circles, and if you have difficulty half-halting to a slower tempo and engaging a collected and expressive trot, then be warned! You can assume that your horse does a passagey trot too often. Dressage training can never develop this kind of trot into a true passage. It also can never develop it into a beautiful extended trot. Therefore, you should never think that you'll get anywhere with that kind of an elevated trot. Its only value is as a circus act for an audience; it doesn't hold any value for you.

I hope I've been able to clarify this for you somewhat. Good luck with your horse!

Chapter 4

Losgelassenheit

In the last chapter, rhythm was the main topic. This chapter focuses on the second basic training concept: losgelassenheit, the synonym for looseness, suppleness, and relaxation. Coby van Baalen and Johann Hinnemann emphasize that this relaxation is something physical, connected with the muscles and other parts of the horse; however, relaxation is also associated with the horse's inner tranquility. This desired inner tranquility and contentment is as important as physical relaxation in the horse's training.

Whether the horse has only been under saddle for a year or whether he's training at Grand Prix level, his training hour should always consist of three stages. These include a relaxation and warm up stage, a work stage, and finally a cool-down stage so that the horse can recover from his efforts. The term "training hour" should not be taken too literally, as a half-hour training session for a young horse certainly can be sufficient. Of course, the rider does not reach the real work stage with a green horse, and the session should often be considered successful if the horse relaxes for the rider. That is often where misunderstandings begin, however. Many people think that getting the horse supple and relaxed is only important for young horses. That is not so. Warming up and achieving a supple and relaxed state is important throughout a horse's entire schooling. "*Losgelassenheit*, which is physical as well as psychological, is the key to success in riding horses," says Hinnemann emphatically and solemnly. "When schooling any difficult exercise, it always must be possible to immediately relax the horse again, at any time, both physically and psychologically."

A content expression should be evident during the greatest effort: This is the meaning of "inner relaxation" or "inner losgelassenheit." Johann Hinnemann pictured on Ideaal during the European Dressage Championships at Goodwood, 1987. They won the team gold and individual bronze medals.

Warm-up and Relaxation

The first goal of warming up and relaxing the horse is a physical one. This includes loosening and warming up the horse's muscles, tendons, ligaments, and joints. Warming up the muscles increases the blood supply to them. Joints take longer than muscles to become elastic; in other words, it takes longer for the joint fluid (synovial fluid) to make the joints flexible.

Warm-up starts with at least ten minutes of walking on a long rein. Marlies van Baalen is pictured here on More Magic. Letting the neck lengthen allows the horse a long stride. A long neck also allows the front legs to move sufficiently forward. In riding, the development of rhythm and losgelassenheit go hand-in-hand.

Marlies van Baalen warms-up Inspekteur at the trot. The mouth at chest height and the nose in front of the vertical is ideal. The hind legs are allowed to step through sufficiently. Notice the muscles at the top of the neck are nicely flexed while the muscles underneath the neck are relaxed.

"If you realize the physical importance of warming up for the horse," says van Baalen, "then you certainly understand the risks to the horse's health if you rarely or never take time to warm up. You risk muscle strains, tendon injuries, or joint problems."

COMMODORE

(Calypso I x Marder), bred by Hermann Huesmann, born in 1978. Commodore was an approved stallion prior to being gelded.

Commodore was already training at Grand Prix level when van Baalen acquired him. The difficulty in being a new rider on a schooled horse is that, quite often, problems from the horse's past show up in the present, and the trainer or rider may not know the exact history of those problems. That was the case with this horse. "Commodore was very fearful," says van Baalen. "The main problem was keeping him supple and relaxed in his work, both mentally and physically. For that reason, I had to work hard to gain his trust as his rider, and Johann had to do the same as his trainer, not only at home, but also at shows. That was really difficult. I ultimately won ten national Grand Prix's with him in Germany. There, I had the advantage of being allowed to ride with a whip in national shows. I didn't really need the whip, but when I carried it, Commodore would submit and focus on his work. A horse with a history stays difficult, but Commodore was the ideal schoolmaster for me because he allowed me to gain show experience. He also gave me the experience of doing real Grand Prix exercises, such as tempi changes and piaffe. I'm still grateful to him for that."

Relaxation and collection are two sides of the same coin, which Commodore is displaying here.

First, relaxation on a long rein...

Then, a rhythmic trot with impulsion...

Commodore is the ideal schoolmaster. His carriage of his legs as well as his body is quite classic in type. "However, his ears tell you that he doesn't have perfect 'inner losgelassenheit,'" says Hinnemann meaningfully.

Finally, the pinnacle of collection: the piaffe.

Warming up, as is often said, begins with at least ten minutes of walking on a long rein or a light contact. Continues van Baalen, "Of course, you don't want to invite an accident on a young, fresh horse that wants nothing more than to get rid of his excess energy. In exceptional cases of exuberant, fresh horses, you may be better off skipping the walk."

As the warm-up progresses, the rider should begin riding at the rising trot. The horse should be ridden with a light contact and in a regular and active tempo on long lines and large circles.

"Active is not the same as hurried or out of control," Hinnemann points out. "A horse gets tense if the tempo is too quick. In that case, you don't have the correct rhythm, which was discussed in the previous chapter. A too-quick tempo causes the horse to tense certain muscles, which is not conducive to achieving suppleness and relaxation."

A too-slow tempo is not good either, says Hinnemann. "A too-slow tempo doesn't invite the hindquarters to step under the horse actively and doesn't allow the horse's back to come up enough," he explains.

Consistently warming up and striving for suppleness and relaxation helps nervous horses become quieter and phlegmatic horses become more enthusiastic and active. "That's just something you learn through experience," Hinnemann says. "The correct, systematic, warm-up work increases the horse's willingness to work, his physical condition for the work, and his inner tranquility." When the horse loses his initial stiffness or tension, he should definitely be cantered in this phase, again on long lines or large circles and in an energetic, working tempo. True relaxation can never be achieved without the canter.

"Many horses relax their backs, allow their riders to sit comfortably, and respond to the driving and restraining aids better as a result of transitions," says van Baalen. "A few trot-canter-trot transitions help many horses really relax. The transitions are also conducive to forming a nicer rapport between horse and rider."

Characteristics

Confirming a pure rhythm and striving for relaxation or *losgelassenheit* characterize the primary training goals of the habituation and familiarization phase—the first year and a half of schooling. When you begin working on a pure rhythm, you enable your horse to move in balance under the rider. Then the horse can "swing," a prerequisite for *losgelassenheit*. Rhythm and *losgelassenheit* are mutually influential. A horse can only move in a pure rhythm if his back swings and his neck and back muscles contract and relax without force. A relaxed horse bends and extends his joints equally, and he appears content.

"Optimum relaxation isn't just a biomechanical issue but also an issue of a horse's inner peace," says van Baalen. "Tension always blocks everything the rider wants. You often see riders who fight against tension. That's a shame. It's wasted energy, and you achieve the opposite of what you actually want. The horse should radiate pleasure in his work; he shouldn't appear constricted."

Several characteristics identify a horse that is both externally and internally relaxed and moves in such a manner under the rider: a content expression in his eyes; relaxed ears; a regularly swinging back; a closed, softly chewing mouth; a calm and rhythmic snorting or blowing; and a quiet tail. "A supple and relaxed horse allows his rider, in seat and psyche, to be supple as well. You can see that right away," van Baalen says decidedly.

Stretching the Neck Long and Low

During the warm-up stage in which the rider strives for *losgelassenheit*, he or she may also practice stretching the horse long and low in all three gaits. The rider should maintain constant contact with the horse's mouth when stretching the neck long and low or letting the horse "chew the reins out of the hands." The neck is usually stretched to chest height, and the horse's nose must always stay in front of the vertical when chewing the reins out of the hands.

"Allowing the horse to 'chew the reins out of the hands' is very useful," says van Baalen. "You just shouldn't confuse it with letting the horse fall on the forehand. As the rider, you determine the 'accordian action' of the horse's neck, which can be stretched and then recompressed. In theory, the rider can bring the horse's neck as low as he wants, as long as it is done at the rider's direction and the horse continues

The rider should maintain constant contact with the mouth when the horse "chews the reins out of the hands" during warm-up.

to carry himself and doesn't fall on the forehand. Stretching the horse's neck to chest height is usually sufficient. Letting the horse chew the reins out of your hands checks if the horse is round through his back and can also improves the way a horse uses his back at the same time. This continues to be important for young horses as well as for Grand Prix horses."

Letting the horse chew the reins out of the hands is not only an indicator of the level of relaxation achieved, but it is also a measure of the rhythm and contact established. It is easiest to stretch the horse's neck, while keeping the contact, on a large circle. The rider should drive a bit more strongly with the leg to keep the hindquarters active and to maintain contact with the mouth in a lower position. For this purpose, it is often better to stretch the horse's back and neck for short, frequent periods rather than for one lengthy session. Over time, riding a horse for extended periods in a low position with his nose ahead of the vertical can cause the horse to lose his impulsion and travel on the forehand. That, of course, is not the intention.

At Every Level

At every level of his training, a horse should demonstrate the desire to loosen his back, lengthen his neck, relax his jaw, and chew the reins out of the hands. "'*Lass ihm dehnen*' is one of my most frequently used instructions during training," Hinnemann says. "*Dehnen* means to lengthen, to stretch. A young horse should want to obviously lengthen upon the rider's every request, and a schooled horse should be no different. That lengthening may only be a miniscule amount, but the desire to do so must be present. The length in the neck allows the horse to step further under himself and through, resulting in more movement, and a longer stride. This is,

There are many ways to relax and make a horse content. Variety is essential for a horse's physical and psychological relaxation and development. Johann Hinnemann at home with Ideaal in 1988, training in the walk.

ARTHUR

(Pretendent out of Rosalie by Liguster), **bred by W.A. Dogterom, born in 1982.**

Arthur was a nice horse to ride with a lot of natural impulsion. Marlies van Baalen rode Arthur in the European Championships for Juniors in Helsinki, where an incident occurred that subsequently negatively affected the rest of Arthur's show career. Before the placings for the international competition were awarded, a marching band came onto the field. Arthur, who was standing in the line-up, spooked really badly. He wouldn't stand still anymore after that.

"Arthur is a completely different horse," says van Baalen. "We've worked with him with extreme patience and care to try to regain his trust, and to quietly make him halt and stand, but to no avail. He was so traumatized by that scare in Helsinki that he hasn't been able to recover. That's how you learn that good and bad are sometimes two sides of the same coin. Some horses don't forget a bad experience. Arthur was super quiet at home but never again at shows. He just wouldn't relax anymore."

Arthur moves with great impulsion. Unfortunately, a bad experience made relaxing him at shows very difficult.

GRENOBLE

(Bismarck x Roemer), **bred by the De Beijer family, born in 1988.**

The *Keur* mare Grenoble earned very good scores on the International Light Tour. That is worth mentioning, as not many mares reach the top in dressage. The reason for this may be that a mare's cycle can be difficult to combine with detail and precision-oriented dressage training. In every instance with Grenoble, there was a world of difference between when she was in season and when she was not.

"You couldn't keep Grenoble on the leg when she was in season," explains van Baalen, "and if she wasn't on your leg, then you couldn't get her to relax. She blocked her body. How well she did at a show really fluctuated because of this. Ultimately, that inconsistency isn't conducive to success at the FEI levels. Now, she's completely been given her due as a talented sport horse broodmare. In 1999, she gave birth to a foal by Ferro; in 2001, a foal by Roman Nature; and in 2002, a foal by Idocus."

The Keur mare, Grenoble.

ultimately, the goal of dressage: to improve the horse's natural gaits. The danger of the neck becoming short during training is ever-present. That's why I constantly emphasize in my lessons that a horse must want to lengthen his neck at the slightest request. Collected exercises or excitement-generating movements, such as flying changes, should still always leave the way open to the horse lengthening and stretching his neck. Only at that point, do you have a horse that performs the most difficult exercises while staying completely relaxed. It's for good reason I've said, '*losgelassenheit* is the key to success,' because you can be certain that every training problem is caused by tension and lack of suppleness."

Psychological Relaxation

Relaxation and suppleness do not necessarily have to be achieved in the arena. Longeing, hand-walking, or free jumping are other useful options.

The *losgelassenheit* that every horse at every stage of his training during every exercise should be able and willing to demonstrate is also psychological in nature; therefore, variety is very important. Sometimes, a walk on the trail appears to be the ideal way to achieve optimum suppleness in a horse.

"A rider should have a plan in mind for the day before he or she starts riding," says van Baalen. "That plan, of course, can be adjusted somewhat, according to how the horse acts that day. Formulate a specific training or show warm-up structure for yourself in advance. Otherwise, riding often deteriorates into a half-hour's worth of purposeless circles without much accomplished."

Hinnemann adds, "A good rider feels what the horse needs, and that can vary from horse to horse and from rider to rider. In general, variety ensures that a horse stays fit and lively as well as content, supple, and relaxed."

Question:

Relaxation in the Trot

I have an eight-year-old gelding that I recently started showing Second Level (Medium Level in the UK) dressage and Level 2 (Discovery in the UK) jumping. He's a big horse: 17.2 hands (1.78 m). I don't really have problems with exercises such as shoulder-in, turn on the haunches, and counter-canter; however, I do have problems keeping my horse relaxed as I ride him forward. I don't have problems with tension in the canter, but I have a lot of difficulty energizing and then relaxing him in the trot. How can I best solve this problem?

Coby's Answer:

Relaxation Exercises

I'm glad that you write that relaxation in the canter isn't a real problem. That's a starting place. There's no reason why you can't first get your horse to relax in the canter before you attempt the trot. Your horse apparently thinks the canter is easy and enjoyable. In the canter, he softens his back, moves under himself well, and evidently, the energy of the canter strides flow through his body nicely. In the trot, he clearly finds it more difficult to swing and loosen his back and keep the movement flowing through his body. Therefore, you should use that canter. Then trot, and try to let your horse follow your hands and chew the reins down to about chest height. Ride mostly in rising trot. Furthermore, most horses really enjoy cavaletti work, which contributes to relaxation. At first, place the cavalettis about three feet, three inches (1 m) apart on a straight line, but eventually, put them on a circle so that you can trot over them toward the inside of the circle (where they're closer together) or towards the outside (where they're farther apart).

Vary collected exercises with calm, forward riding where you let the horse chew the reins out of your hands, riding shoulder-in in the sitting trot and then going straight ahead in rising trot, again letting him chew the reins out of your hands. Do these exercises in both directions. In the beginning, practice only very small segments of sitting trot and a lot of rising trot so that you can relax and as a result, your horse can, too. Tension in your seat can also lead to tension in your horse.

You can also leg-yield or ride a few strides of half-pass—don't do too many; it will give your horse the opportunity to tighten his back—immediately followed by riding straight ahead in a relaxed rising trot. Increasing and decreasing circles is another great exercise for control and relaxation. Ride a lot of walk-trot transitions trying to stretch your horse with the downward transition and collect him a bit with the upward transition. Think of your horse as an accordian that you can compress and extend. Be sure to vary your horse's work so you can keep his attention and he continues to submit to you.

Keep the trot work brief in the beginning and repeatedly ask for the canter, the gait that relaxes your horse. Ride forward in the trot-—but definitely not fast—so that your horse can find his balance and, ultimately, can relax, too. Ask a professional to check your tempo. You may be riding too fast.

You can also facilitate the horse's ability to relax and trot forward with looseness and suppleness through his body by other means, such as turning him out, longeing him a little prior to riding, or taking the time for a half-hour trail ride. Relaxation can be achieved in many ways, but don't make too big of a deal over it. Relaxation doesn't exist in isolation: It needs to be coupled with a pure rhythm and an even stride, connection and contact, and straightness on two reins. In short, relative to your horse, relaxation needs to be part of the entire training scale and the topics discussed in this book. Focus on and be content with the parts of your horse's training that are going well, and relaxation in the trot will follow. I wish you success!

944

Confirming Horizontal Balance

Contact

Impulsion

Chapter 5

Contact

Many riders spend their entire lives wrestling with their horse's contact. The horse is too heavy in the hand or too light; his head isn't quiet; he's stiff and against the hand; he tilts his head. Plenty of different problems! This is not the case, according to Coby van Baalen and Johann Hinnemann, when you see contact as one of the six basic concepts of a jumping or dressage horse's training. Good contact always interplays with the concepts already mentioned—rhythm and losgelassenheit—as well as with the concepts yet to be discussed—impulsion, straightness, and collection. All of these together result in a horse that is nice to ride. The rider's aids go through optimally. This chapter discusses why good contact does not have to be a life-long struggle.

Most people are accustomed to thinking of the concept of contact as the sensitive and light, elastic connection with the horse's mouth that the horse offers in response to the rider's request. This is a somewhat limited view, according to van Baalen and Hinnemann. "I feel that contact with the horse is actually affected by three points," says van Baalen. "I believe the first contact point is your leg. Your leg should be in constant contact with the horse, and the horse needs to understand what it is saying. Even the horse's basic understanding of that is already a type of contact. The second point is your seat, which includes your seat, knee, and hip. You use your seat to give aids to your horse, which your horse answers by responding with movement. You can also call that response 'contact.' Finally, you have the rein contact, which arises from the connection between the mouth and the rider's hand. That is the third contact point." Hinnemann adds, "I really want to emphasize that a rider first rides a horse with the legs and seat; then come the rein aids, as a support to the seat and legs. These three things together subsequently determine the quality contact that leads to the complete harmony and understanding between the horse and rider."

lance and contact e easy for the allion Ehrentanz. dden by Coby van alen, Münster, 1999.

According to Hinnemann and van Baalen, contact originates from three areas of contact with the horse: the legs, seat, and hands. The three-point contact is clearly evident in the photo. Horse and rider are in balance. Ferro demonstrates a "live" contact.

Connection and Contact

Van Baalen and Hinnemann clearly want to emphasize their shared view that a good contact with the mouth can only occur if the rider also has good contact with the seat and legs. The rider maintains contact with the driving aids and strives for a rhythmic and relaxed, forward-moving horse. The horse takes the bit and draws, so to speak, on the rider's hand. In this way, contact is created.

"Indeed," Hinnemann says, "people also say that the horse seeks the contact and the rider enables the horse to find it."

"In other words," van Baalen adds, "the rider asks with the connection, and the horse answers with the contact."

A good contact provides the horse with the security he needs to regain his natural balance under the rider and to move in that balance in all three gaits. When the horse is ridden with his neck stretched long and low, the neck is extended like an accordion, and the horse should absolutely not be pulled together. "The end result should always be an elastic contact," van Baalen says, "in which the poll is the highest point and the ears are level. This applies to the lateral movements as well."

INSPEKTEUR

(Darwin out of Doornroos *Keur*, preferent from the lineage of Amor x Officier), **bred by the late Mr. J.H. Dorresteyn, Coby van Baalen's father and Marlies' grandfather, born in 1990.**

The KWPN stallion Inspekteur has naturally good contact. He finds it quite easy to respond to his rider's three-point connection of leg, seat, and hand with contact. "As a three-year-old," van Baalen says, "you could already look at his conformation and neck shape and tell that he would have a nice, willing mouth and go easily on contact."

His rider, Marlies van Baalen, finds that a big advantage. "It's really ideal when a horse naturally has a nice neck conformation with a sufficiently long, top neck muscle," continues van Baalen. "Then a nice contact happens almost by itself. Inspekteur always comes on the bit. He never gets too light in the hand or too tight in the neck. He never gets behind the vertical. That, of course, makes him great to ride."

This is contact. The horse answers the three-point contact of leg, seat, and hand. The shape of the neck is the result of the driving aids.

Marlies van Baalen became the Dutch Young Rider Champion for riders 21 and under on Inspekteur, Nijmegen, 1999.

BABOON

(Sire: Uniform out of Tineke by Pantheon *Keur*), **bred by Alb. Moors, born in 1983.**

The mare Baboon was sometimes too hot to let the rider use the leg and seat to send her forward into the contact.

Baboon was a hot mare. That made her often difficult to manage, especially in the beginning. Her movement would become too hurried with too little self-carriage, which lures the rider into using the hand to control the horse rather than driving the horse from the leg into the hand.

"If you kept your leg off her, things went from bad to worse," says van Baalen. "Then the contact would never be consistent. At that point, she stopped accepting the leg at all. We then had to figure out how to get her on the leg. If she completely accepted the leg, then I could finally get around to riding. As a result, the too light contact stopped. I had to pay constant attention to the contact and driving aids while training her. If the contact isn't right, nothing is right."

Baboon had incredible talent for piaffe and passage. Therefore, it is not surprising that she ultimately achieved Grand Prix level.

The Logical Outcome

In van Baalen and Hinnemann's view, a good contact is the logical outcome of riding forward and always striving for good rhythm and relaxation in the horse's movement. The horse develops a sure and constant contact out of this contented carriage and *losgelassenheit* (both physical and psychological in nature, as described in the previous chapter).

"A pleasant and light contact is subsequently the most important means of improving a horse's impulsion," says Hinnemann. "A rider can straighten a horse by riding him forward with impulsion. A straight horse can finally achieve a degree of collection under his rider. In that way, the circle becomes complete: Rhythm, *losgelassenheit*, contact, impulsion, straightness, and collection—they all work together. Finally, these qualities ensure that the horse is totally receptive to all the aids; we call that *durchlässig*, completely on the aids."

The ideal contact requires constant connection with the rider's hand. This applies even in the free walk, as Marlies demonstrates here on the stallion Inspekteur.

Of course, the rider's hand must always be present to achieve the ideal contact. Says Hinnemann, "A horse will come behind the bit if he has too little connection with the rider's hand. Furthermore, the horse won't come on the bit anymore if he's allowed to take the bit in such a way that he can also readily back off it."

Coming Away from the Bit

"Coming away from the bit?" When you read the German expression for the first time, "*Abstoszen vom gebisz*," you may be inclined to think that this "coming away" is a major fault. However, coming away from the bit is decidedly not the same as not taking the bit at all. In this instance, Hinnemann views coming away as a sign that the horse completely accepts the bit. The horse allows the impulsion of his hindquarters to flow over his back and through his neck to a closed but "living" mouth. He trusts the bit completely. At the same time, the horse lightly and almost imperceptibly comes away from the bit. The rider notices the contact become even nicer and lighter and the driving and restraining aids are optimally communicated. The horse doesn't display any resistance in his body. The horse accepts the bit as part of his body, so to speak. Thus, coming away from the bit is actually the optimum contact a rider can have with the horse's mouth.

Ultimately, this state of perfect contact will help the horse and rider team in the future when both are further advanced in their training, not as an irrevocable thing that doesn't require further thought, but as something in which higher degrees of perfection can continually be achieved.

"I could almost write a separate book about the ideal degree of contact in coming off the bit," says Hinnemann. "It's an on-going development process that is not visible to the eye but is definitely felt by the rider."

Not With the Hands

The rider should never force contact with the hands. "Everyone has pulled on the reins to get a horse's head and neck in the right position," van Baalen says, "but to no avail. It's always detrimental to the horse's schooling. It may look nice—such a proud, round neck—and the horse may even come up a bit. However, if the shape of the neck is not the outcome of the driving aids and a good contact with the seat and legs, then it's meaningless, because the hindquarters aren't active and the back isn't swinging, allowing the movement to flow through the body. Using the hands from front to back always immediately causes the hind legs to step under the horse less actively. This should be a red flag to every rider. The hind legs not stepping through should never happen, because the goal of dressage is to improve the gaits! Contact and a particular neck shape should always be the outcome of the driving aids, a horse that moves in the correct rhythm, that shows contentment, and that moves with a supple body."

A correctly ridden horse seeks the contact himself. He approaches the bit with confidence.

Conformational Shortcomings

Of course, achieving a good contact is not always easy. A rider's hands can often feel a horse's every problem. "I always say that with riding," van Baalen states, "and definitely with the contact, you actually fight against conformation flaws. Horses with flawed necks, for instance—too long or too short or too high set—also have difficulty bending. In those cases, achieving a good contact will be far more difficult than with a horse that has a well-formed neck. This applies to horses with difficult mouths, too. If the hindquarters are weak, the horse will have difficulty with self-carriage behind, and that is also usually a contact problem with the rider's hand. If the horse's conformation contributes to an unsteady or difficult contact, and that's the case ninety percent of the time, then the rider needs a lot of extra patience to improve the conformation by making the horse stronger and properly muscled. It takes quite a bit of time to develop—to make usable, in any case—a part of the horse that nature didn't gift athletically."

In general, we can say that strong, heaviy-built horses usually take a heavier contact than light, hot-blooded types. This is just a function of the horse's type.

The Right Bit

Another reason for contact problems can be an improperly fitted bit or a bridoon and curb that don't lie comfortably in the horse's mouth. Most riders know the general guidelines: A bit fits properly and is adjusted to the proper height if it is approximately two-tenths of an inch (1/2 cm) wider than the mouth and if the corner's of the mouth are not pulled up too high. However, a bit adjusted too low is not good either, as it will often bump against the eyeteeth. The thinner the bit, the sharper the effect. A double-jointed snaffle allows the tongue a little more room than a single-jointed snaffle.

"I must honestly say I've noticed that there's still little attention given to properly fitting bits," says Hinnemann. "Even at the higher levels, I often see horses in double

The stallion Zonneglans (Le Mexico out of Rhodos by L'Espoir x Erasmus), as a six-year-old in 1987. In 1986, Zonneglans was rejected as a breeding stallion for his line. "He had nice movement, but he would get nervous at shows and that would sometimes cause problems with the contact," explains van Baalen.

ROMAN NATURE

(Rohdiamant out of Esprina by Ehrentusch), bred by Johann and Willi Lenzen, born in 1995. Dam, Esprina, is a full sister of the dam of the stallion Florestan. In 1992, sire Rohdiamant became champion of the stallion *Keuring* in Oldenburg. In 2000, his approved son, Roman Nature, became reserve champion of the five-year-olds at the World Championships for Young Dressage Horses.

The obvious ease with which Roman Nature performs all movements contributed to him winning the reserve championship for young horses at the World Cup.

"Roman Nature's strength is his incredibly good ability to collect without one seeing any change in the contact," says van Baalen. "He has naturally good contact."

"What's more," adds Hinnemann, "he's compactly built, light, and supple: the perfect horse for a young, slender rider like Marlies. A horse and rider team should be pleasing to the eye, and I think Marlies and Roman Nature are an ideal combination."

Roman Nature, ridden by Marlies van Baalen, demonstrates natural contact in all his tempo changes and transitions.

EHRENTANZ

(Ehrentusch out of Fantasie B by Frühlingsrausch), bred by Ludwig Schüring, born in 1990.

The stallion Ehrentanz excelled in his score for rideability during the stallion performance testing. "That's not so incredible, such a high score for rideability," says van Baalen. "That stallion has no physical shortcomings and therefore can easily do everything the rider asks of him. Ehrentanz has powerful, energetic movement, and his hind legs move with the correct forward tendency. That makes balance and contact easy. As riders, we're always fighting against nature's shortcomings. The smaller the shortcomings, the more effectively you can train."

bridles with much too long a shank, with the curb so wide that it's pulled through the horse's mouth, and with a twisted chain. Seeking advice on the correct use of the double bridle is not shameful; on the contrary, it's a smart idea."

Previously, almost everyone rode with a single-jointed, fat eggbutt snaffle; nowadays, the thinner, loose-ring snaffle can be seen everywhere. "You shouldn't worry about fashions and practices," urges van Baalen, "rather, experiment a little with bits to see which your horse goes in best. Some horses like thick bits; others like thin bits. Notice your horse's temperament as you train him and take that into consideration."

Temperament

Van Baalen believes that contact is sometimes a matter of temperament and personality. One horse is more nervous than another, and that can also have repercussions on contact at times you do not expect it, like at a show.

Van Baalen has always ridden a lot of stallions. The stallion Zonneglans (Le Mexico x L'Espoir), bred by J. Bekkers in St. Oedenrode, could surprise his rider with respect to contact. "Zonneglans could suddenly get very nervous," explains van Baalen, "and then all at once drop the bit. He would then start rattling the bit and pull his tongue up. Sometimes he would even get his tongue over the bridoon and curb. Then I would have to exit the arena, because I no longer had any control. This was in the mid to late 1980's, and at that time, I still didn't have enough experience to solve that problem. Now, if I'm riding a stallion that suddenly does a similar thing, I know I have to give the reins forward so that the horse has the freedom to get his tongue back under the bits. It also helps to set the bit a little higher in the mouth. That's how you solve a temporary problem with the contact."

A rider striving for optimum contact must consider his horse's conformation as well as his temperament. However, if a rider always goes back to the basics of rhythm and relaxation and making contact with the leg, seat, and hand, he will sooner or later receive the answer from the horse that he's been waiting for: Contact!

Question:

The Double Bridle

I have begun to compete at Third Level (Advanced Medium in the UK) and would like to start riding my horse in a double bridle. How do you choose the right double bridle for your horse and how often do you train in it? My horse has a sensitive mouth, so a bridoon seems too thin to me. He also has a small mouth so he can't accommodate much bit. I've tried a thick bridoon and curb, but he was really afraid of it. Am I actually required to ride in a double bridle at Third Level?

Coby's Answer:

The Right Double Bridle

Many misunderstandings surround the double bridle, but there are many advantages to using it. One misunderstanding is that the double bridle is required when showing at Third Level. That's not true. Another is that the judge thinks your horse has problems with his contact if you don't ride with a double bridle and that you'll get higher scores for riding with one. That is also untrue. A judge values a nice, "living," flowing contact that is quiet but also "breathes." You can achieve that contact perfectly with a snaffle, and you should confirm that before you even consider using the double bridle. In general, you should make sure that your horse is very steady on both reins and confirmed in his simple changes, counter-canter, tempo changes, and transitions without any resistance is his jaw and neck. If that's the case, then you can consider learning to ride with the double bridle.

The bit rests on the toothless areas of the mouth: the bars.

Learn to Ride

I intentionally say "learn to ride" because there's a second misunderstanding commonly associated with the double bridle. Learning to ride with the double bridle is grossly underestimated by most riders. It is far more difficult than most people think! The rider needs to have more sensitivity. Don't underestimate the action of the curb. The shank of the bit, or the lever arm, where the rein is attached, directly affects the top of horse's neck, just behind the ears. The leverage action of the curb means that a small aid given by the rider is felt much more intensely by the horse. It's for good reason that some people use a "baby curb" when learning to ride with the double bridle. The baby curb has a shank four-tenths of an inch to one inch (1–3 cm) long, which has less leverage effect than a longer shank. It's a compromise for both horse and rider, and perhaps it's a useful transition bit for you.

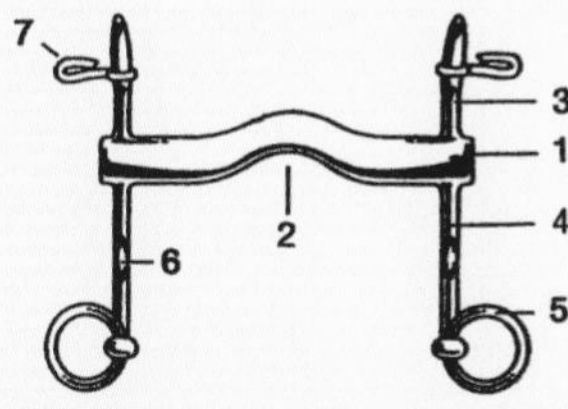

The parts of the curb bit.

1. *Mouthpiece*
2. *Port*
3. *Upper cheek*
4. *Shank*
5. *Bit ring*
6. *Space for a lip strap*
7. *Curb chain hook*

The bridoon and curb chain
The loose-ring bridoon of a double bridle is usually thinner than a normal loose-ring snaffle. In general, Coby van Baalen has had the best experiences with the double-jointed, loose-ring snaffle.

The Right Double Bridle

In general, an average bridoon and curb bit of normal thickness, are the best. Other types of curb bits have their advantages, but at the same time, have disadvantages. A curb with a high port, for example, seems horse-friendly. A high port

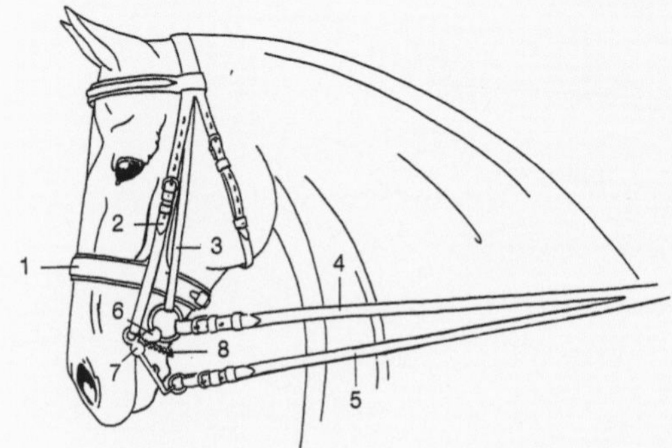

The parts of the double bridle

1. *Cavesson noseband*
2. *Curb cheekpiece*
3. *Bridoon cheekpiece*
4. *Bridoon rein*
5. *Curb rein*
6. *Bridoon bit*
7. *Curb bit*
8. *Curb chain*

allows plenty of room for the tongue, right? However, you have to consider that the horse gains tongue room at the expense of room elsewhere, such as the bars. This curb acts more severely on the bars than the average curb, precisely because the tongue is entirely free. A normal port spreads the pressure over the tongue and bars. "Normal," is therefore always best, with an average port and shanks of reasonable length. The rules state that the shanks may not exceed four inches (10 cm), but this is very long,and requires a rider with very sensitive hands. Instead, choose a shank about half that length. The diameter of the bridoon ring may be as large as three inches (8 cm). I also think this is very large. This certainly does not make for a pretty picture on a horse with a small mouth. The bridoon and curb should visually look good in the horse's mouth; then it usually also feels good.

Consult the USA Equestrian (British Equestrian Federation) regulations to learn what bits and bridles are permitted for dressage competition. A cavesson noseband is required with the double bridle; flash nosebands are not allowed.

Furthermore, the double bridle requires a curb chain. I've never had a new girl at the barn who immediately could put on a double bridle without making a mistake. In 99 out of 100 cases, the curb chain is twisted. The same is true at shows, so always pay close attention. The chain hooks that are attached to the curb are different on the left and on the right sides, so also pay close attention when replacing one of the hooks. The curb chain, which lies against the chin groove at the same height as the curb, is essential for the curb to work. See the illustrations. The curb chain may be covered with a piece of leather or rubber for sensitive horses.

For my own feel, the double-link bridoon has proven itself over time. The double-link bridoon provides the advantage of tongue freedom, as discussed earlier. In addition, you should check that both bits are made of the same material, as this is also stipulated in the rules. Every tack shop should also be able to tell you that. If you can, first borrow a double bridle from someone, perhaps your instructor, and then buy one once you know what fits your horse.

Adjusting

You should take a step back in your horse's schooling while he's adjusting to the double bridle. Do only exercises that are well confirmed and give your horse confidence in his new bridle. Do a lot of rising trot, stretching circles, figure eights, and serpentines so that you can learn how to gather up the reins smoothly and always take the correct length on the new outside rein and take the new inside rein a bit shorter through the turns and in the other direction. The curb rein should hang with a light loop through all this work as you maintain contact on the bridoon rein. Don't forget, as you can easily use too much curb rein. Some riders find it helpful to use two different reins made from different materials: for example, a fabric jumping rein for the bridoon rein and a thinner, leather rein for the curb.

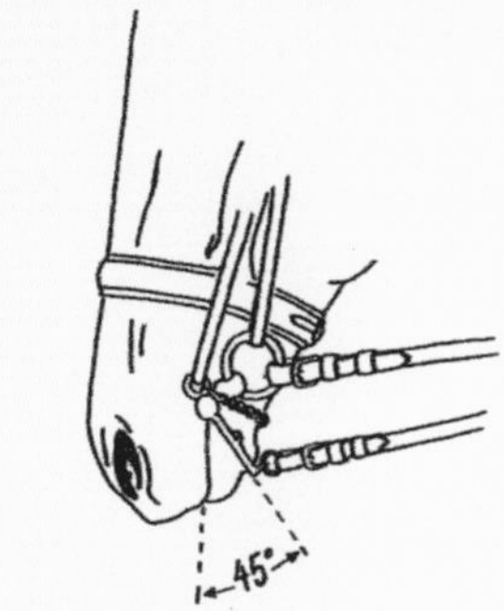

1 **Correct:** *When the rider takes up the snaffle and curb reins, the angle of the curb shank should form approximately a forty-five degree angle with the mouth.*

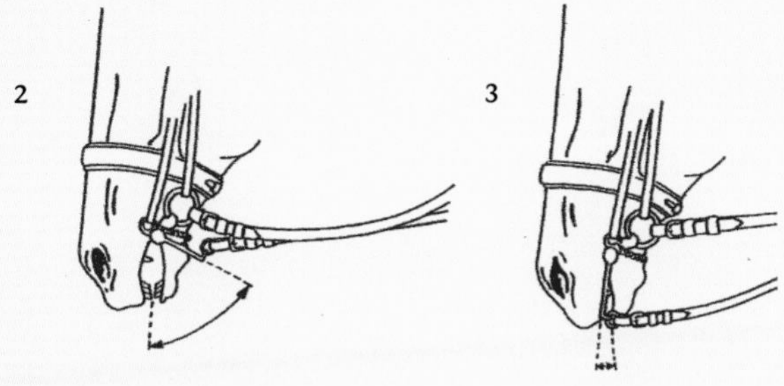

2 **Incorrect:** *The curb angle is too great. The curb chain is attached too loosely; as a result, the curb acts too strongly on the corners of the mouth and too little on the bars and poll, where it is intended to act.*

3 **Incorrect:** *The curb chain is attached too tightly, allowing the curb to act too severely.*

Don't use the double bridle more than two or three times a week when the horse is first learning to get used to it. Some horses are very hot and react to the double bridle with little confidence. With such horses, you may even consider warming up for half an hour with the snaffle rein only before taking up both reins. If your horse is very obedient and enjoyable on the trail, then in this learning stage, ride him easily in the double bridle when you go on the trail. Stay off the reins. This will help your horse gain confidence in his new bridle, and it will help him seek the contact again later.

Darwin in a correctly fitted double bridle.

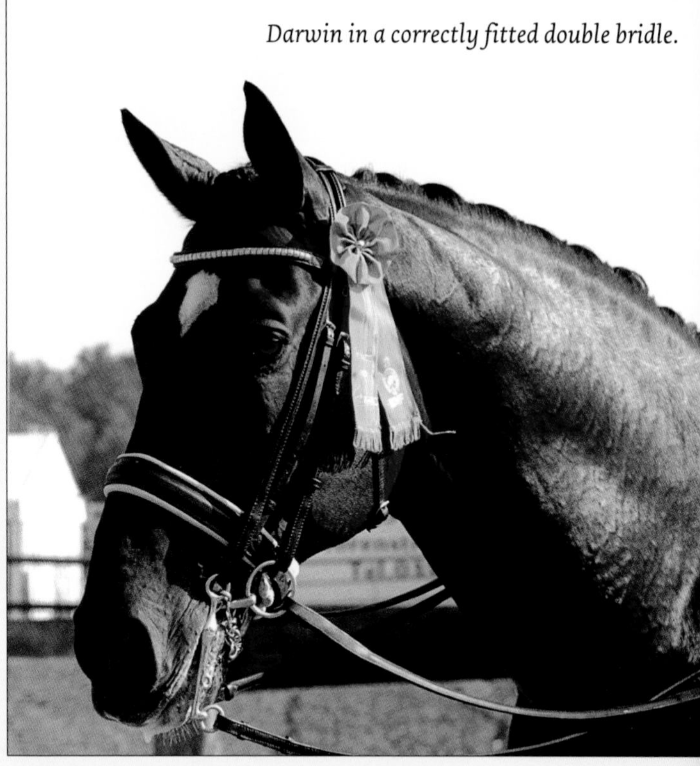

Confirming

After the initial learning stage, you will naturally build up your work with the double bridle until you are again at the level you were previously, asking for some collection and compression in the transitions, and other such things. However, continue to use the curb rein carefully. It's difficult to say, without seeing you and your horse, if you should, after an adjustment period of several weeks, continue to alternate between the double bridle and the snaffle. I prefer to train all my horses in a snaffle all the time, with very few exceptions. In contrast to the lower levels, the double bridle is mandatory at the FEI levels. I also feel I need to stay in practice riding with the double bridle to attain and continue to confirm that very nice contact required at the upper levels. Given the rather busy show and exhibition schedule at my barn, I usually ride my upper level horses in the double bridle. Everything takes time and practice, but practice makes perfect. I wish you success in this new stage of your riding development!

World Online

Chapter 6

Impulsion

Many riders think that impulsion, also known as schwung, is something inherent in the horse, that this swinging movement of a horse with a loose back is something your horse either has or does not, and that there is not much you can do to improve it. Coby van Baalen and Johann Hinnemann insist that this is not so. You can indeed develop your horse's impulsion with good basic training. A horse that really swings his back and moves impressively with loose, supple gaits does not happen by itself. This desired way of moving is closely connected to good rhythm and contact as well as the horse's established losgelassenheit. All of these characteristics of a properly working horse act reciprocally upon one another, as mentioned throughout this book. The one strengthens the other. We have already discussed the concepts of rhythm, losgelassenheit, and contact. In this chapter, we will talk more about impulsion, which adds extra shine to the movement.

Training a horse, as discussed, consists of three stages. The first stage, habituation and familiarization, focuses constantly on the horse moving in the correct rhythm and achieving complete relaxation. After approximately a year and a half, the horse and rider are ready for the second stage. This stage focuses on confirming the horse's horizontal balance under the rider and stimulating greater activity of the hindquarters. Contact, as discussed in the previous chapter, is key during this stage as well as is developing impulsion.

:oby van Baalen on Weltino, Brakel, 2001.

Theory

To begin, here is an excerpt from a text on riding theory:

"*Schwung* is the flow of the energetic impulsion from the hindquarters through the complete forward movement of the horse. A horse moves with impulsion when he picks up his legs energetically, and in the moment of suspension, swings his body and limbs well forward."

This photo series of Heruto (Doruto x Enfant x Amor) is a lovely example of how the impulsion developed in the extended trot is maintained and used for beautiful, active collection. Notice the hindquarter joints and forehand elevation when the hind legs bend more.

Extending...

Half-halting on the hindquarters...

And collecting into a piaffe with impulsion.

DARWIN

(Sire: Tangelo xx out of Jolanda by Darwin out of Rosetta by Leopold GP x Colibri GP), born in 1985, bred by Roel Hagedoorn in Wierden. In 2001, Roel Hagedoorn was honored as Breeder of the Year by the KWPN. Examples of horses bred by him include Darwin and his half-brother, the approved stallion Vasco (sire: Gag), out of the same mare, Jolanda.

Darwin, Inge Fokker's horse, is living proof of impulsion in movement, just like Sonja Gademann's horse, Jup. These horses naturally have a powerful, active trot and an uphill canter. "If you look at Darwin's conformation," van Baalen explains, "you can see that he's able to carry weight on his hindquarters and to turn impulsion in his movement into carrying power; in other words, collection." Look at the example of Inge Fokker and Darwin in the extended trot, many years ago at a Dutch championship in Haaksbergen. The contact is correct; the impulsion is evident. Both qualities are, in turn, the foundation for straightness and collection.

In 2002, Darwin and Inge Fokker's daughter, Wendy, became the Dutch National Champions among juniors (eighteen and under) and were selected for the Junior European Championships, where they contributed to a bronze medal for the Dutch team. "Darwin is the ideal junior horse precisely because of his natural impulsion and very correct basic gaits," asserts van Baalen.

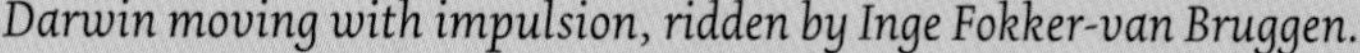

Darwin moving with impulsion, ridden by Inge Fokker-van Bruggen.

And Darwin, once again, as schoolmaster for daughter Wendy Fokker, who can make wonderful use of the natural impulsion Darwin likes to demonstrate.

The rider begins to ride with impulsion "through the forward drive stimulated and completely controlled by the rider." This impulsion develops the actual beautiful supple and swinging movement throughout the horse's entire body, as *schwung* "transmits the optimum impulsion of the hindquarters to the horse's total movement."

"That lovely elastic movement arises when a horse really swings from his hindquarters," says van Baalen.

"Based on the descriptions of the concepts of impulsion and *schwung*," continues Hinnemann, "the walk appears to be a gait without impulsion. The walk, of course, should be active and come from the hindquarters; however, it is a striding movement without a suspended moment. It is precisely in the suspended moment that a horse develops swing. A relaxed horse that moves with an elastic back and offers a light contact can swing in the trot and canter. In this way, the horse can demonstrate impulsion."

Many riders tend to associate the concept of impulsion mainly with extending and riding forward. However, impulsion is very evident in the collected exercises. "You get impulsion in lengthening that you subsequently take with you and maintain in collection," explains van Baalen. "Your collection should be so swinging that you can get extra impulsion and *schwung* from it for another lengthening. At any rate, that's the ideal picture."

Let us go from theory to practical application. Impulsion is achieved by activating ("mobilizing," as Hinnemann likes to say) the hindquarters. A rider activates the hindquarters by doing many short tempo changes and transitions. "It's about activating and checking," van Baalen says. "For example, a rider can activate the horse's hindquarters in the walk by moving him laterally two or three strides and

Delphine Meiresonne with Top Yellow. First, she gets impulsion in the extended trot. Next, she maintains the impulsion generated through the half-halt and then collects more into an expressive trot.

FINESSE

(Aktion out of Wendelien, *Keur* sport performance by Onyx), **bred by Marjan Dorresteijn, born in 1987. Finesse is a half-sister to Habibi.**

Of all the qualities a horse can have, sometimes an exceptionally strong temperament is the most important quality. That was true for Finesse. Finesse earned wonderful *Keuring* scores before she earned dressage scores. For example, she earned an IBOP score of AA95 points and, as a four-year-old with a Chronos foal at her side, became *Keur* and general champion riding horse in Utrecht. Under saddle, her best quality is also her most difficult quality: Her strong temperament gives her an iron will. Van Baalen gave her sister, Marjan, many lessons on Finesse and says, "Finesse works for you happily and does her very best. However, you also have to consider her temperament: she is willful. Her pride and willfulness translate into her outstanding show arena presence." Finesse's determination ultimately saved her life. She caught an unusual virus after her first Grand Prix test, and the veterinarians at the Faculty for Veterinary Medicine had actually given up on her; however, Finesse's iron will, even then, helped her recover.

From the time she was born, Finesse was a remarkable, proud-looking foal. That proud foal is still clearly evident in Finesse's body attitude as a mature sporthorse.

JUP

(Democraat x Joost), **bred by B.E. Kleinheerenbrink, born in 1991. Jup quickly became the most talked about young horse in the Netherlands because of a sizzling career, winning every possible title in every class.**

This beautiful photo of Jup and Sonja Gademann in the extended trot during the 1998 Dutch Championships in Nijmegen, clearly demonstrates impulsion. Jup also demonstrates good use of his joints. He picks up his hind legs actively and moves them forward.

Jup is very electric and very elastic, a big advantage in schooling dressage. "Jup is remarkably light-footed for such a big horse," claims van Baalen. Jup was initially a stallion, and even after he was gelded, he continued to demonstrate often intense stallion characteristics for quite some time. Fortunately, his rider, Sonja Gademann, could handle him well.

"You should try to turn a disadvantage into an advantage," states van Baalen. "If you know how to put his aggressiveness on the right track, you can benefit from his power and big, swinging movement."

Commodore performing a half-pass with rather little impulsion and too little forward/upward drive and expression.

then trotting forward, preferably on a large circle. After doing these walk-trot transitions a few times, try transitioning to the trot without activating the hindquarters more by pushing them laterally. This is checking. If the horse is correct, he then moves just as actively from the hindquarters as he did earlier with the lateral steps. In this way, you develop impulsion."

A horse that moves with impulsion allows his rider to sit comfortably. This occurs because his relaxed back muscles absorb motion from the hindquarters. Essentially, the horse's movement flows into the rider.

Conformation

A horse with a compact and uphill build is definitely an advantage. "A well built horse allows the rider to easily develop elastic gaits," says van Baalen, "to bend the joints, and to work the horse. Take, for example, Sonja Gademann's Grand Prix horse, Jup. That horse is built nicely uphill and has the correct joint angles in his hindquarters for developing power and impulsion from them. The first stride when stepping forward from behind is always essential. Then the horse steps forward, or he does not. Jup does that naturally, and he did that from his very first moment under saddle. It is still essential that Sonja ride him from back to front, but the result is simply better than it might be with a horse with less pleasing conformation."

BAS

(Sire: Rinaldo out of Flika by Robert O Lee ox), **bred by F. Pompen, born in 1983.**

Bas was originally Stal van Baalen's jumper that all the working students rode to earn their jumping certificates for the riding instructors course. However, Bas' breeding was evident: His temperament and non-stop energy also made him an excellent dressage horse.

"Bas was limited in his movement," says van Baalen. "However, he's the perfect example of a horse that was successfully trained to Grand Prix level because of his strength and willing attitude. He even developed impulsion in his passage and was always active. 'Ears forward and go': That was Bas' motto!"

Due to his willing attitude and natural impulsion, Bas was transformed from a jumper into a dressage horse.

WELTINO

(Weltfeuer out of Pagena by Polany), **bred by Heinz Dieckhoff-Holsen, born in 1997. Weltino is related to the famous Swedish dressage horse sire, Chagall, through the Swedish dam, Renja, by his sire Weltfeuer. That makes him related to Liselott Linsenhoff's Olympic Champion, Piaff, and the Grand Prix stallions Chirac and Gauguin de Lully.**

Weltino is a horse with natural impulsion. He is big and very elastic with a great deal of natural balance.

"If you sit on Weltino once, you immediately know what's meant by 'let the horse carry you.' What you feel is incredible: Weltino just wants to take the contact with your hand and swing forward under you. He's a horse that's always in front of your leg! Really, I've never ridden a horse before that gives you this feeling," says van Baalen. "As the rider, all you have to do is direct him. Later, of course, the balance will need to be brought more to the hindquarters."

The horse's natural way of moving also plays a part in this aspect of developing impulsion. "There are just some horses that naturally use their hindquarters powerfully, and then there are horses that just as naturally use their motor less," says van Baalen. "A rider, however, shouldn't rely too much on the horse's natural abilities. You see, if your horse doesn't use his hindquarters well, then you should automatically focus on activating his hindquarters. You should be very attentive to that. However, if your horse does use his hindquarters well, then you should consistently ride him from back to front and continue to set him on his hindquarters; otherwise, these kinds of horses will indeed use their hindquarters less over time."

Mistakes

A horse that swings through his back in the trot and canter moves his hocks forward and upward energetically after pushing off. The horse definitely does not pull his hocks up or push them out behind prior to moving forward. It is important that a horse actively completes the movement behind. The hind leg hoof print should always go over the front leg hoof print. As the horse achieves more collection with the hind leg joints bending more, he will pick his legs up higher. A slow, passagey trot coupled with the horse lifting his legs up high is always wrong. "An amateur can easily get tricked into thinking that this passagey trot is good," says van Baalen. "However, it's an undesirable way of moving. The movement must be upward and forward. The joints should never be pulled up and back at the same time. The horse should also move more quickly in collection, not more slowly. The hind legs are in maximum activity during collection; in other words, they are bent and quick."

Another mistake van Baalen often sees riders make is practicing collection too often while not concentrating on other aspects of correct riding. She finds this especially true among riders who want to quickly accumulate high scores so that they can advance to the higher levels. "Repeatedly practicing half-pass usually doesn't improve the half-pass," van Baalen points out. "You can't maintain the rhythm and impulsion. That's why you should always alternate collected movements with riding forward. Get impulsion, get *schwung*, and then try to keep that in your lateral work."

Hurrying the horse is another common mistake when working overzealously on impulsion. "The horse should always carry the movement and not run," says Hinnemann. "Developing impulsion mobilizes the hindquarters so that they really work. With a horse that tends to 'keep the brakes on,' it's a good idea to canter energetically forward a good distance, until that resistance disappears. In general, however, work on a lot of short tempo changes: Ride forward a few yards (meters), then collect for a few yards. This is a much better way to develop impulsion than chasing the horse forward for long stretches."

Question:

Warming Up

I have a five-year-old horse that I show at First Level (Elementary in the UK). I know that everyone says this, but things do usually go well at home. My test scores, however, are rather inconsistent. Sometimes my horse suddenly goes too deep in a test, while he didn't do that at all during his warm-up. Sometimes he moves swingingly through a test; other times he seems dead, and I can't get him forward. Sometimes he suddenly acts spooky, while he wasn't spooky at all during his warm-up, and I usually deliberately warm up close to the show arena. I wonder what I'm doing wrong. Should I warm up differently?

Coby's Answer:

Warm Up with a Plan

I could devote a whole separate book to your question about warming up. I see riders make so many mistakes at shows. I'll talk about that in a minute. First, I want to discuss the course of your whole show day. You write that your horse suddenly goes too deep. Perhaps he was already tired. A young horse such as yours is often very excited at a different location and full of bravado. However, after expending such emotional energy, he may suddenly be tired. You have to watch out for that and take frequent walk breaks so that your horse still has spark left for the show ring.

In addition, you need to ask yourself what happened at home before you left for the show. Did you upset your horse's daily routine? In other words, could he eat, drink, and urinate as usual before you loaded him in the trailer? Were you busy for hours washing, braiding, wrapping your horse's legs, packing your gear, and dressing yourself before you actually left for the show? Did your horse stand waiting for you the whole time in the barn aisle with his legs neatly wrapped? These things take a young horse so out of his routine that he's already tired and stressed before he even gets to the show. Most horses won't urinate in a trailer. A horse that hasn't urinated can get so uncomfortable that he'll hardly move anymore. That's why you should learn your horse's behaviors and try to recognize when he's tired or stressed.

Form a Plan

Now I want to talk about warming up. The most common mistake is warming up without a plan. You know your horse better than anyone else does. You know how much time it takes to get him really loose and swinging forward, and you know how much time you need to get him attentive, concentrating on you and the aids. Therefore, always ride with a plan based on your experiences and exactly how you ride at home, and do not deviate from that plan.

I often see riders who constantly look around and stop for lengthy conversations with everyone they know. Of course, it's nice to visit with people; however, talking with acquaintances is best done after a show. Chatting prevents you from a focused warm-up and proper preparation. Furthermore, don't be tempted to just ride really big lines in a huge warm-up area. That'll make it really difficult if you then suddenly have to ride your test in a 20 x 40 meter arena. Visualize an arena with long and short sides, and ride applicable straight lines and circles within those boundaries. Keep the designated right-of-way rules in mind when warming up. If another rider is coming toward you from the opposite direction, then always move to the right. If you're walking your horse, then keep well to the inside of the track so that others can easily ride passed you.

In addition, I also see riders, particularly at Third Level (Advanced Medium in the UK), who get nervous if well-known trainers or instructors are watching. These riders want to impress those watching, so they start doing a lot of extended trot in the warm-up arena, for example. As a result, they enter the show arena with a tired horse. Or they make their horse quasi-impressive by compressing him until he does piaffe-like steps, which results in a jigging horse that will no longer walk in a relaxed manner. There's no benefit to doing these things! It doesn't matter whether the

Marlies van Baalen, on Habibi, concentrates on the lines of her test one more time while a groom removes Habibi's wraps and team trainer Jürgen Koschel watches. Marlies went on to become Junior European Champion (eighteen and under) at Hickstead in 1998.

Some shows go better than others, despite preparations being exactly the same. This is true for everyone. No one gets in top shape and becomes successful without a lot of hard work, although it may appear that way to onlookers.

The apple does not fall far from the tree, as can be seen here. Coby van Baalen concentrates on her Olympic Grand Prix test in Sydney. Her trainer, Johann Hinnemann, and groom, Irene van Seggelen, prepare Ferro for the test.

Queen or an Olympic champion is watching you. Stick to your plan when warming up, and don't see or listen to anything around you except for your own trainer, test reader, or helper.

As you warm up, you should already know which parts of your test are solid and which parts are not. If your horse falls over the outside shoulder in the leg-yield, for example, then only warm up with a couple of steps of leg-yield and then ride forward. This way you make your horse wait for your new lateral aids. If you've just started showing at Third Level and your horse still gets really tense in the flying changes, then you should consider not doing any changes in your warm-up. Just do the preparations for a change and see if you can remain relaxed in the arena. The first halt and rein back are usually not the best. Definitely remember to practice that in your warm-up. However, don't spend all your time practicing one part of your test. Training should be done at home. Your horse won't get better leg-yielding ten times in a row right before your test; he's more likely to get worse.

Another thing you should do is plan break time. It is much more beneficial warming up in focused ten minute increments with walk breaks on a long rein in between—keeping contact with the mouth and making the horse walk with energy—than going for a half-hour non-stop. I must say that, in general, the walk is unfortunately practiced very little during the warm-up, although the First Level (Elementary in the UK) tests already require the horse to demonstrate differences between the medium or extended walk and the working walk. Therefore, you should practice the walk.

Fit and Focused at the Start

Neither you nor your horse should be "out of gas" and dead tired before you enter the show arena. You should set aside time for applying extra fly spray, wiping your boots, putting on your jacket, and taking off your horse's boots or polo wraps, without this creating any tension.

Some riders immediately feel different when they have on gloves or a jacket. Those riders may feel better warming up wearing their glove and jacket.

Unfortunately, not all shows are well planned. Therefore, you should teach your groom to check from time to time if the show is running on schedule. Use the last few minutes to put your horse together and get him on the aids again. As you ride around the arena, check two things: First, that he's listening to your leg and will go forward. Ride him forward a few strides. Second, check if he'll come back. Half-halt him nicely, transitioning to the walk or halt, if necessary. Then, throw your whip down if you ride Second or Third Level (Medium or Advanced Medium in the UK) and begin your test focused and alert. Continue to think ahead and ride well in the arena. Don't let a mistake get you down; just keep riding for the next score. You can win a class with your final halt!

There are always surprises. Your horse spooks at a duck flying from a canal. Your horse is distracted by the noise and thumping of someone unloading another horse from a trailer. The worst mistake you can make is allowing these things to affect your equilibrium. Don't look at what your horse is distracted by. Sit relaxed and continue riding so that your horse refocuses on you. Know your test so that you only rely on your reader as a memory support. At home, with your test book in hand, you should really try to visualize riding every step of your test without letting your mind wander for a second. This is an excellent concentration exercise to help prepare for such a moment. You'll discover this visualization isn't so easy sitting in a chair in your living room, and it is far more difficult when you're actually riding. Consistent concentration isn't so easy.

Finally, practice makes perfect. This also applies to riding in shows. I wish everyone who wants to go on to big shows or perhaps participate in a qualifier or championship much success. If things don't go so well, there will be other chances. Remember that this is a hobby. You do it for the enjoyment. Shows are great fun; however, they never outweigh the daily enjoyment you get from your horse or pony. No judge's score could ever change that!

Developing

Balance on the Hindquarters

Straightness

Collection

E
V

Chapter 7

Straightness

When rhythm, losgelassenheit, contact, and impulsion are reasonably confirmed in a young horse, then it is time for the next step: developing more balance on the hindquarters. Straightness is the main focal point of this chapter, as it is an essential condition for collection and the horse's true self-carriage.

Everyone has seen pictures that explain why a horse is not straight by nature. These pictures show that a horse's hips are wider than his shoulders. Therefore, if you continuously ride a horse along a wall or on a track, he will tend to gravitate toward the wall with his outside shoulder and outside hip. His hindquarters will move slightly to the inside because of his broader hips. In other words, your horse will move crookedly.

Natural Crookedness

There is another cause of natural crookedness in horses, Johann Hinnemann says. "Every horse naturally has an easier side," he explains. "Just as every person is naturally right or left handed, so is every horse. We continue to emphasize that a rider's job is to gymnasticize his horse, to attempt to alleviate this natural crookedness through correct work. A crooked horse can never move entirely in balance and always has an escape door through which the energy can't optimally flow through from back to front. He can never correctly carry weight on his hindquarters. That's why straightness is a very essential part of a horse's training."

Straight as an arrow in the canter, the forehand perfectly positioned in front of the motor: the hindquarters. As a result, the horse is perfectly on the outside rein. Marlies van Baalen and Inspekteur in their upper Third Level (Advanced Medium in the UK) championship dressage test at Levade, 1997.

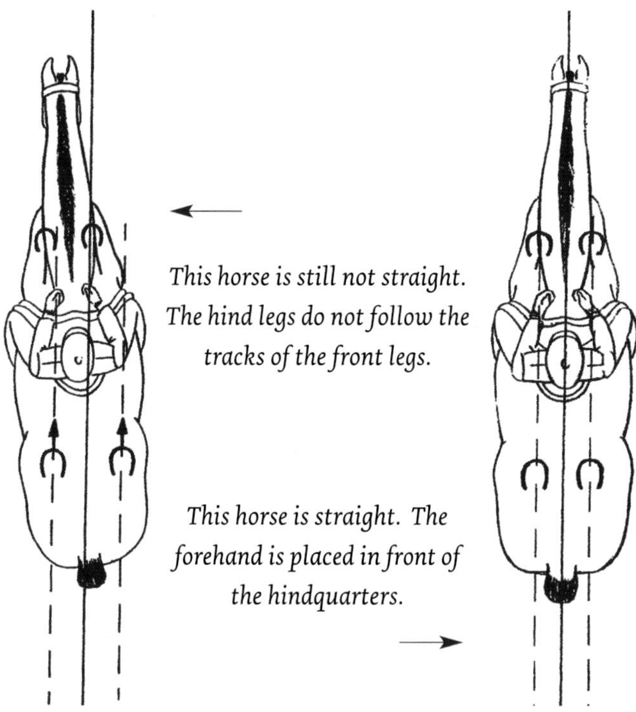

Straightness

"Reite dein pferd vorwärts und richte es gerade."
"Ride your horse forward and make him straight."

This statement by the classical master, Gustav Steinbrecht, is often quoted in riding texts. It is also a very simple summary of how to school a horse. In short, the horse's energy must come from his hindquarters. Applying any aids that work from front to back is decidedly wrong. A straight horse is straight on straight lines and as bent on curved lines as those lines may require.

"You start straightening a young horse to some extent as soon as you begin riding him," says Coby van Baalen. "Even in a Training Level (Novice in the UK) test, you can get low scores for halting crookedly, falling out on circles, and wandering off the centerline. However, the straightness defined in riding theory really begins when a horse has learned the first stage of training and is in the stage of developing carrying power and learning to balance on his hindquarters. This is the stage we will now discuss."

Theory: Moving Crookedly

Imagine that a horse is tracking right and moving crookedly. His hindquarters are somewhat to the right toward the inside. His right hind leg is therefore not under his mass, does not carry weight, and avoids bending. The left shoulder—closest to the wall—automatically bears more weight and the rider will feel more weight in his hand on the left rein than on the right rein. The horse is then braced and too tense in his neck muscles on the left side. This is the "round" side. The real problem, however, is the "hollow" side—the right side on which the horse does not completely take the bit. The crooked horse moves with his hindquarters right, to the inside, and

NOBLE CASPER

(Sire: Downland Folklore out of Ulanka by Dennenoord by Sadat ox), **bred by H. Bekkers in Mariahout, born in 1987.**

Belgian rider Delphine Meiresonne's European Champion pony, Noble Casper, distinguishes himself, according to van Baalen, by his lovely way of moving straightly. "There are really few ponies that are truly straight," says van Baalen knowingly, "but Noble Casper is one of them." Noble Casper excels in exercises such as simple changes. "However, he excels in those precisely because he's straight!" says van Baalen. "Casper does very lovely transitions from the collected canter, rocking back onto his hind legs, into the walk, during which he stays totally straight. He bends his hind leg joints in these transitions without trying to escape or getting crooked. Because he is so beautifully straight in the orientation of his hind legs, he also does lovely, light, and elevated transitions from his hind legs. Then he scores 8's and 9's on his tests. During the European Championships, which he won, he definitely distinguished himself from other horses precisely by this way of moving."

Noble Casper is a textbook example of straightness.

Notice the slightly bent neck and the ear position of 1998 European Pony Champion, Noble Casper. This is straightness.

Practicing staying straight in the transitions. Instructor van Baalen watches. (European Pony Championships, Le Touquet, 1998.)

responds insufficiently to the rider's right leg. Correct gymnastics should condition the right hind leg so that it moves straight under the horse's mass, also causing the horse to take more right rein. As a result, the tension on the round side disappears by itself.

Practical Application: Shoulder-In

If you really think about the horse's natural crookedness, then you understand that a rider must consider the width of the horse's hindquarters and always focus on placing the forehand directly in front of them. The hindquarters are the motor.

The most important exercise for improving carrying power and straightness is shoulder-in. "In your training," says Hinnemann, "you can begin with asking your horse for a little inside bend. Then you can ask a bit more and do shoulder-fore, and then even a bit more for the shoulder-in. In a correct shoulder-in, the inside hind leg follows the path of the outside front leg. In other words, the horse moves on three tracks: one track for the outside hind leg; one for the inside hind leg and outside front leg; and a third track for the inside front leg."

By bringing the forehand to the inside, you do not make your horse crooked on the other side; in contrast, you make him straight because the hindquarters are now activated and can no longer avoid the carrying action. The rider can also ensure that

Horses that are equally developed and straight also demonstrate these qualities in lateral movements such as shoulder-in and half-pass. These horses take an even contact, hold both ears at the same height, and do not tilt their heads. (World Equestrian Games, Rome, 1998.)

Before the rider can ask the horse for the extended trot, she first has to straighten him. Then she must continue focusing on that straightness during the extended trot. (World Equestrian Games, Rome, 1998.)

the horse brings his hindquarters under his mass and takes the rein better on the hollow side with leg-yielding.

More Exercises with Shoulder-In

Many horses avoid carrying themselves by bringing their hindquarters to the inside when asked for a canter depart or during transitions from and to the medium canter. "With this too," van Baalen says, "it's the rider's job to make the horse stronger so that he carries himself. That's why a rider brings his horse into the shoulder-fore position before cantering. The shoulder-fore allows you to get the horse properly on the outside rein. Then you can give with your inside hand so that the horse's inside hind leg can stride forward nicely. As a result, the inside hind leg has to carry more weight, and the horse can stay straight during the canter depart. This is also true for the transition from the medium canter back to the working or collected canter: stay in shoulder-fore position. Only then do you compel the hindquarters to bear weight."

Many horses become crooked in the flying change. Here too, the "magic exercise," shoulder-in, applies as a remedy. "Let's suppose you're in the left lead canter," Hinnemann says. "As you prepare for the change, imagine that your horse is already in a shoulder-fore position or shoulder-in to the right. Then apply the aids with your seat and leg in the moment of suspension. In this way, the new inside hind leg is free to stride forward powerfully, and you can keep the hindquarters as straight as possible."

You can even develop a pirouette from shoulder-in, van Baalen says. "You do a circle at the canter in a shoulder-in-like position and decrease the circle, continuing in the shoulder-in position," she explains. "That way, the inside hind leg comes nicely under the horse's body. A pirouette is only successful if the hindquarters really will bear weight and do not try to evade doing so by going sideways. I want to say, as a caution, that the first time I showed Prix St. Georges, I kept practicing pirouettes. Of course, you shouldn't do that because you lose the canter. You have to constantly vary this exercise with riding forward to continue to get impulsion."

A nice exercise for attaining straightness in the canter is the counter-canter. A horse is practically unable to move crookedly in the counter-canter along the wall because he does not have any room to bring his hindquarters to the outside. "The rider should continue to concentrate on staying in that shoulder-fore in the counter-canter, too," says van Baalen. "Riders frequently forget this when doing serpentines. You see their horses falling out in the turns and the accompanying changes from the canter to the counter-canter. That's why you should concentrate on staying in shoulder-fore position, continuing to control the horse with the seat, two legs, and the reins. That's important for maintaining straightness."

Always in the Track

Some riders think of the term "straightness" as just being straight on straight lines. This is not correct. As Hinnemann says, "A straight horse's hind feet move in the impressions of his front feet. A horse should also be straight on the path of a circle: He should again follow the path of his front feet." "As a rider," adds van Baalen, "you should try to concentrate on what is happening behind you. Don't become fixated on that head and neck set before you. The action must happen behind your saddle, as that's where you find the carrying power. The straighter and more equally both hind legs follow the path of the front legs, the stronger the hindquarters become. The rider must mobilize the hind legs behind the saddle and ensure that the horse moves straight in order to confirm his balance in motion and impulsion, which are maintained and used for still more impulsion and for the ultimate goal of training: collection."

IDOCUS

(Sire: Equador out of Eretha Keur by Zonneglans), bred by Christine McCarthy, born in 1990. Idocus was one of the best dressage sires in North America until he returned to the Netherlands to begin a European dressage career under his rider, Marlies van Baalen.

Idocus' straightness is immediately apparent in all his Grand Prix movements. Hinnemann and van Baalen think he is a textbook example of straightness.

"Idocus is naturally so straight that he can do canter pirouettes to the left and right with exactly the same ease," says van Baalen, "and he can make those pirouettes precisely the same small diameter in both directions. Even in his flying changes, he's straight as an arrow. The same goes for his passage. An uneven, swinging, or irregular passage can always be traced back to not developing both sides of the horse equally; as a result, the horse can't carry himself. With Idocus, all of this is perfect."

Idocus in a uniform passage. A uniform passage is only possible when a horse is optimally developed equally and is straight on each side.

Question:

Too Heavy or Uneven Contact

My seven-year-old gelding is going quite well and shows at Second Level (Medium in the UK) dressage, but sometimes he's a bit tight in his poll and jaw. What exercises can you recommend?

I have another question: My sister has a six-year-old mare, who also shows at Second Level and has always been strong in the mouth and heavy in the hand. Over the last few months, she has been hanging extremely heavily on the right rein. She will hardly bend, or she won't bend at all to the right. If I take on the left rein, she will bend her neck far too much to the left, and won't take any contact at all on that rein. The dentist has already examined her and couldn't find anything unusual. What can we do to make her better?

Coby's Answer:

Straightness

First, I want to encourage both sisters. Don't despair, I'm absolutely sure that the majority of horses showing at Second and Third Level (Medium and Advanced Medium in the UK) dressage are crooked to varying degrees or too tight in the jaw on one or both reins. You both should take comfort in knowing that you're not alone in this problem.

Now, let's find a solution. I must say that for amateurs like you who usually only ride one horse, acquiring good contact and a straight horse are the most difficult things to do. This is because you become crooked with your horse and are so accustomed to it that it is very difficult to break the pattern. I still have clear memories of times when I thought I couldn't get through a turn on a certain horse, that I'd run into the wall or some such thing. So I know exactly how you feel!

What can you do to break that pattern?

You can start by trading horses with another rider at your barn. Get on another horse and feel if he's straight and on both reins. Let your sister, someone at your barn, or preferably, your instructor ride your horse a few times. The main thing is that you get a new feel.

Improve the Hindquarters

Now, I'll talk about the exercises. A horse that is crooked in the contact is also crooked behind the saddle. When mounted, try to concentrate on what's happening behind you. Both hind legs must take equally large strides and must step energetically under your horse. He needs to learn how to bend around your leg and obey that right leg.

That improvement must come from the hindquarters.

The second horse in your question hangs on the right rein and won't take any weight on the left. Focus on staying relaxed on the right rein as you warm up. For example, start your warm-up by doing lots of changes of rein. Continue to do large figure-eights or half-circles to the left and right. Try not to bring the horse in with the heavy inside rein when circling to the right; instead, give immediately with the inside rein as soon as the horse comes onto the circle so that the horse takes the left (outside) rein. You can then increase and decrease circles tracking to the right. Push your horse into the outside rein when you increase the circles.

Counter-canter can also help. Do counter-canter left lead, with little bend, tracking to the right, and try to relax the right rein. Even bend your horse gently to the right in this same left lead counter-canter. Play with the contact; be creative, staying light and quick with your rein aids. Lateral work can help, too. The rider can shoulder-in to the right to encourage the right hind to step under the horse's body. While doing this exercise, the right rein must stay relaxed and the rider must drive with the right leg into the left rein so that the horse takes the left rein. You can also do renvers. For example, position your horse in shoulder-in left and then change the bend to the right for renvers. Try to be especially aware of your right hand so that you remind yourself to constantly relax it. Be very quick and alert in giving the reins, as if you're massaging the corners of the horse's mouth.

Another good way to help horses that are "stiff" in the poll and jaw as well as horses that are crooked is through correct longeing. The stiff horse can learn to accept the contact more easily with side reins. The crooked horse can learn to take the left rein by making the left side rein somewhat shorter than the right. The heavy right rein isn't the biggest problem; it's the too light left rein and the associated hind leg not stepping under the horse that are the real issues.

I wish you much success with your horses. Don't think that everything will be solved in a week and that you'll never have to do anything further. That's not how it goes! Good contact will continue to play a part in all your training, just like good rhythm in the gaits, *losgelassenheit*, and all the other topics discussed in this book. A horse's training is never an established fact. It remains a process with ups and downs, but that's precisely what makes it exciting.

Chapter 8

Collection

Six basic concepts comprise the successful education of a dressage or jumping horse: Striving for rhythm, losgelassenheit, a nice contact, impulsion in movement, straightness, and finally, collection. The goal of dressage is to make a horse carry more weight on his hindquarters. Thus, in this chapter, we have finally come to the sixth concept: Collection.

"If we talk about straightness and collection, then we're finally talking about the specific specializations of a dressage horse," says Johann Hinnemann emphatically. "Everything else—keeping rhythm, suppleness, impulsion, and striving for the optimal contact—applies to every riding horse, even a trail horse, because it's not enjoyable to ride a horse through the woods if he won't carry himself, or constantly pulls the reins out of your hands, or isn't responsive enough to your seat."

Collection

Impulsion and straightness make it possible to encourage a horse to carry more weight on his hindquarters. This action involving the hindquarters is called "collection." The horse lifts both hind legs equally in the direction of his center of gravity and puts them down again. The horse's increased power allows him to bend the joints in his hindquarters more, which is called *hankenbiegung* in German. As a result, the horse lowers his croup somewhat as he simultaneously lifts his forehand, and his trot or canter strides become more elevated through the increased bend and stretch of the hindquarter joints.

A horse achieves collection through the rider's application of half-halts. Following is the definition of a half-halt, as stated in the rules of the International Federation for Equestrian Sport, the F.E.I. (article 408).

The half-halt is a hardly visible, almost simultaneous, coordinated action of the seat, the legs and the hand of the rider, with the object of increasing the attention and balance of the horse before the execution of several movements or transitions to lesser and higher paces. In shifting slightly more weight onto the horse's quarters, the engagement of the hind legs and

[…]by van Baalen [tr]aining without [st]irrups on Ferro in [Sy]dney, Olympic [G]ames, 2000.

Coby van Baalen on Olympic Ferro performing his specialty: a piaffe with the joints bent in his hindquarters, and lightness and elevation in his forehand. Johann Hinnemann is in the background. (Stallion Show, Zwolle, 1999.)

the balance on the haunches are facilitated, for the benefit of the lightness of the forehand and the horse's balance as a whole.

That is stately language, which can also be simplified. A half-halt is the short, simultaneous action of the weight, leg, seat, and rein aids, which are always followed by relaxing and giving the hand. Half-halts are often done one after the other, until the horse becomes attentive, active, and lighter in the hand. A full halt is always the halt—*parade* in German—that leads to immobility, which is usually preceded by a series of half-halts.

"We've continually said that every action of the hand that is too strong hinders the horse's gymnastic development," Coby van Baalen says. "Every obstruction imposed by the hand has an immediate negative effect on the length of the stride. Now, you may say, 'yes, but you want shorter strides in collection.' Indeed, but the strides should not only get shorter but should also become more energetic and elevated because the horse is bending his joints. Forcing the horse with the hands only shortens the strides and blocks every movement from flowing over the back. This is wrong. The rider can shorten the stride while still keeping the horse coming through from back to front by applying the rein aids with feel and simultaneously driving forward and keeping the horse's rhythm. The horse should also bend more in the joints so that he actually bears more weight on his hindquarters."

OLYMPIC FERRO

(By Ulft out of Brenda by Farn x Prefekt), bred by H.J. Gerrits, born in 1987.

When the KWPN breeding stallion Olympic Ferro made his spectacular debut in 1997 in the international dressage world, resulting in the team silver medal and an individual sixth place at the World Cup in Rome, 1998, there was one thing for which he was highly praised above everything else: his classic manner of collection. "Ferro really 'sits' in the collected movements, such as the pirouettes," says Hinnemann. "He brings his weight entirely overly his hindquarters by optimally bending all the joints of his hips, hocks, and ankles. As a result, we see a complete 'uphill' picture and, at the same time, lightness of the forehand."

"A horse that piaffes and does pirouettes in this manner is a true champion. We haven't had this kind of a textbook example of classical theory in years," wrote Eric Lette of Sweden, technical chairperson for dressage for the International Federation for Equestrian Sport, the F.E.I.

Ferro, ridden by van Baalen, displays a trot with self-carriage and energy during their appearance at what is the ultimate goal for many trainers and riders: the Olympic Games.

MORE MAGIC

(Maraschino x Rosenkavalier x Angelo xx), bred by Ludwig Dufst, Gronau, born in 1992.

More Magic only won when he was thoroughly *losgelassenheit*. Although spectators could hardly notice at times, his rider could definitely feel a difference. "More Magic can sometimes be internally nervous, which is barely visible," van Baalen says. "But I definitely feel it! He is so uncomplicated as a gelding and so obedient that he does everything that's asked of him. Nevertheless, when he's nervous, I feel his attention continuously slipping away, which then affects the contact. Everything is ultimately connected. His inner calmness and relaxation improve if I take him to several shows scheduled closely together. Only then do I get the correct collection, allowing More Magic to really bear more weight on his hindquarters."

More Magic in Aachen, 2002.

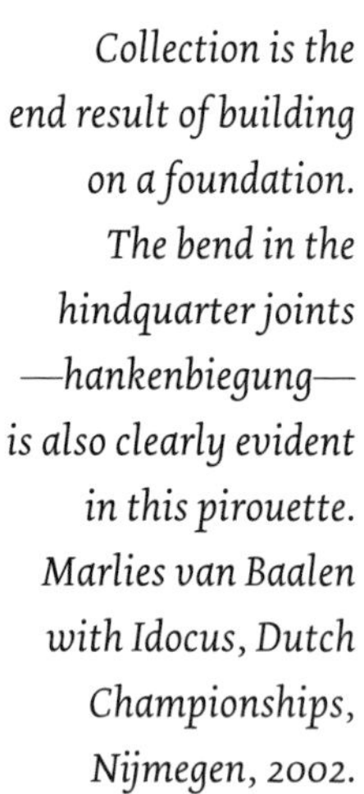

Collection is the end result of building on a foundation. The bend in the hindquarter joints —hankenbiegung— is also clearly evident in this pirouette. Marlies van Baalen with Idocus, Dutch Championships, Nijmegen, 2002.

Impulsion is Necessary

Chapter Six offered a series of photos of van Baalen on Heruto, in which it could be seen how the forward impulsion of the extended trot ultimately resulted in energetic collection in the piaffe. Impulsion is essential to and an absolute condition of collection. "The impulsion of a moving horse must flow from the hind legs over a swinging back to the horse's mouth and back to the hind legs without any hindrance," says Hinnemann. "Small, fine, rein aids allow this same impulsion to flow back over the horse's loose, swinging back. The rider can only actually influence the hind legs when the impulsion flows back and forth over a swinging back without any resistance, and the impulsion in the movement has been established with a correct contact and a straight horse. Then the rider can further encourage the hind legs to bend and bear weight in order to achieve the desired collection."

This book has already discussed the aids and exercises required to ultimately achieve collection. Typically, correctly ridden transitions initiated by the seat and leg, and tempo changes are the exercises used to get a horse to finally compress and extend

Coby van Baalen in piaffe on Biraldo (Sire: Rinaldo). In the schooling session pictured, Biraldo indeed had learned the piaffe; however, he is still not bringing his hindquarters under his body enough. As a result, his forehand lacks elevation.

his body like an accordion and ultimately, to collect. "Here's a word of caution which has already been given several times," warns van Baalen. "Collection means that the movement of the hind legs quickens. The strides become smaller and more elevated as a result of the joints bending. Therefore, collection can never involve the horse simply slowing his movement. A slow, passagey trot has nothing to do with collection."

Willingness to Work

From everything mentioned above, it seems clear that collection can only be achieved if all the qualities discussed earlier are present. "A house without a foundation will collapse," Hinnemann says. "Without rhythm, contact, suppleness, impulsion, and straightness, you don't build collection. Rhythm mistakes, tension, contact problems, all mean that you haven't laid the foundation of your schooling well enough. Then the horse loses expression. Instead of developing and improving his natural abilities, the horse can lose all of his motivation and all of his willingness to work. Collection is the final result of building on a foundation. However, you need to check that there are no cracks in the foundation because that repair work always comes first."

Conformation

Some horses have difficulty with collection due to their build or temperament, while others find it naturally easier. "Horses that are a bit hot or have a lot of Thoroughbred blood are often easier to collect. They are naturally more active, and they transfer their motivation into always wanting to go. If they are well-schooled, they usually bend the joints in their hindquarters easily," says van Baalen.

Horses with little Thoroughbred blood, and perhaps those with long, straight, hind legs or a straight, somewhat old-fashioned croup and stiff hindquarters, have more physical difficulty bending. "You may also find that a horse entirely shuts down in protest," van Baalen says. "That's easy to understand. Hindquarters with little angle have to bend quite far before they bend as much as hindquarters that are naturally more angled. I want to emphasize that a rider should never exaggerate or force a horse. Don't invite protest. Don't overly compress a horse that already has difficulty collecting. Leave the door open a bit and always give the horse room to go forward."

Just as not every person is a sprinter with long muscles, or a weightlifter with thick, short bundles of muscles, not every horse naturally has the all qualities needed to develop athletically into a Grand Prix horse. However, a horse's temperament and willingness are also very important. "There are certain stallions that, even when bred with simpler mares who have less than perfect conformations, produce foals that are always motivated to work," states van Baalen. "With patience and correct schooling, you can go quite far with these types of horses. The stallion Doruto has continually passed on the desire to collect. It's for good reason that at least eight of his direct descendants have become international Grand Prix horses. I've also observed this with the jumper we bred, Bas (sire: Rinaldo). He's never scored an 8 for his extended trot; however, he was ultimately able to do all the Grand Prix work. You can come quite far with horses that always want to work, even if they have physical shortcomings. This is definitely rewarding as a trainer."

In the end, conformation and temperament influence the quality of collection. Commodore doing a pirouette, Münster, 1992.

Van Baalen on Commodore in a very classical piaffe with his hindquarter joints bent.

Horses that have learned collection through thorough, systematic training, can rather easily be motivated by inexperienced riders to do an exercise requiring the highest collection. Claartje van Andel discovers she can do a piaffe on Commodore, much to her surprise.

HERUTO

(Doruto x Enfant de Normandie x Amor), bred by C. Nel, born in 1989, died in 2001.

As a result of being a stallion, Heruto had difficulty concentrating his entire life as a sporthorse, making contact often problematic. "Nevertheless," says van Baalen, "Heruto made it to Grand Prix, mainly because he inherited a talent for collection from his sire, Doruto. He really could collect! Even if he wasn't paying attention, you could still collect him."

Ultimately, all of van Baalen's efforts were in vain. Heruto did not pass the KWPN stallion performance inspection as a result of his poor, distracted behavior. A new opportunity awaited him as a breeding stallion when he was ready for Grand Prix. Then there was another disappointment: He was infertile. The van Baalen family decided to geld him then, thinking that his behavior might improve. However, an incurable injury ended his life. These things, unfortunately, are also part of a life with horses.

Van Baalen on Heruto, who at the time of the photo in January, 1996, was temporarily affected by a pigment disorder. He must have inherited this from his grandsire Amor, who was known for these types of temporary pigment discolorations. The pigment spots later disappeared.

Question:
Seat Exercises

Before my pregnancy, I was ready to start showing at Third Level (Advanced Medium in the UK). Even when I was sixteen weeks pregnant, I competed at Third Level once because I wanted to do it so badly. At that time, I discovered that I couldn't sit well anymore. In the meantime, I have a healthy child, and I've been back in training for a month or two. I'd like to start showing again at Third Level and hopefully move on. However, I still have difficulty sitting quietly. This, of course, affects the way I give half-halts and my horse's level of contentment. Are there exercises I can do to improve my balance and strength, and my ability to sit quietly? I really need help: My horse responds badly when I upset his balance. He reacts immediately by getting tense, running away, becoming fearful of the bit, among other things. What can I do?

Coby's Answer:
Seat Exercises

My instructor, Johann Hinnemann, is always surprised at the lack of attention given to seat exercises. A quiet, independent seat is always the foundation for good riding. This quiet, independent seat isn't something that you acquire once and then have forever. On the contrary, you have to continue to practice and reconfirm your seat. In Germany, you even see many top riders who warm up at a show without stirrups. These are the best riders in the world; however, they continue to confirm their quiet, independent seats up until the start of their tests. I must say that Johann made me ride without stirrups everyday for weeks, even during the quarantine period in Sydney at the Olympic Games.

Every morning after I wake up, I start the day by doing some warm-up gymnastic exercises on the floor. I flex and stretch a bit, loosen my back, bounce a little with my legs. Any physiotherapist can give you suitable warm-up exercises, specially designed to help you warm up your muscles and your back while you're on the ground. I can further imagine that in your situation you would do extra stomach exercises to strengthen muscles that have weakened and stretched as a result of your pregnancy.

Next, I recommend you do seat exercises on the longe line. Don't think that something like this is childish at your level. Your horse must be tacked up correctly with side reins so that he uses his back and allows you to sit nicely. The person longeing should keep the horse moving forward in a quiet tempo, allowing you to focus on sitting. Consider that sitting quietly is not the same as sitting stiffly; you have to swing with your horse. Sit on your seat bones—you can feel them if you sit on your hands—tilt your pelvis, allow your hips to loosen, and swing with the movement. Allow the person longeing you to constantly correct your position; that's necessary. Have your saddle checked just to be sure it still fits.

You can find typical seat exercises in many books; otherwise, your instructor should certainly know a number of exercises very suited for you. In any case, you should definitely ride without stirrups at planned times and focus on your seat. Even when you ride alone, off the longe line, you can often introduce riding without stirrups. This requires discipline, but you'll be rewarded.

It is completely logical that your horse reacts to your imbalance. You would like your horse to respond to very small aids that you give with your seat, weight, and legs, such as your half-halt. Your horse may misunderstand what your imbalance means; as a result, he becomes unsure and responds with tension, tightening, and so on. You'll see the balance probems become a thing of the past if you reaffirm your ability to sit with your horse's movement.

Hinnemann made van Baalen ride daily without stirrups, even while training in Sydney during the long quarantine period.

Six Practical Steps

Flying Changes

Chapter 9

Flying Changes

We have not discussed any single exercise in depth in this book. We will make an exception for the flying change because it can demonstrate very well the importance of systematic and cohesive training according to the six key concepts as described in this book. We will now outline the practical application of the six steps through flying changes.

Flying changes are a known obstacle for many horse-rider teams who have reached Third Level (Advanced Medium in the UK). "I get an incredible number of questions about the subject of flying changes," Coby van Baalen says. "I want to reassure everyone who is struggling with this issue: you are not alone. However, I immediately want to add that you shouldn't wait too long to seek help if you're having problems. There is no shame in getting professional help. In addition, try to practice changes on a well-schooled horse in the meantime, so that you can develop more feel for applying the aids at the correct moment."

Now, let us proceed with the changes. Before we start discussing how to do them, we first want to recap the training system Johann Hinnemann and van Baalen use, as this cannot be emphasized enough.

Six basic concepts constantly play a part in a horse's entire training. These concepts are rhythm, *losgelassenheit*, contact, impulsion, straightness, and collection. With three- to five-year-old horses just started under saddle, the emphasis will be on confirming a correct rhythm and *losgelassenheit*, which are essential for any advanced work. Later, when the horizontal balance is confirmed under the rider, then the rider can build on the established rhythm and relaxation by working mainly on a correct contact and developing impulsion. *Losgelassenheit* leads to the development of a sure contact. A light, pleasant contact with the mouth can subsequently improve impulsion. Riding forward with impulsion facilitates the horse's straightness. For the average horse the time comes when he can shift his balance to his hindquarters. The horse must really carry weight on his hindquarters, and the training can then emphasize straightness and collection. A horse can only collect if he is truly straight.

hann Hinnemann is true "gefühlsmensch," man who is nstantly ntemplating s feelings.

The concepts are ultimately interconnected, and all the concepts are equally important to a more advanced horse. For example, a horse can only collect correctly if he does not have any problems with rhythm. One cannot happen without the other.

It is important to keep this underlying classical theory in the back of your mind when you want to do a correct flying lead change. "I've often said that a rider should never confuse riding dressage with training a horse to do tricks," says Hinnemann. "That can never be the goal of dressage training. Training a horse in dressage means developing a horse gymnastically. It means careful guidance, in which the horse must be fully developed, his performance potential tapped, and his health maintained, leading to great harmony between horse and rider. This is quite a lot; however, it is the starting point for everything a rider wants to achieve with a horse."

When

On average, the rider will first attempt the flying change when the horse is between the ages of five and seven, the period in which the rider usually works on confirming the horizontal balance under saddle and focuses on perfecting the contact and impulsion. "A very experienced rider may teach his horse the flying change sooner," admits Hinnemann, "especially if he notices that his horse is more or less offering it. However, we're not talking about the exceptions; we're talking about the rule. The rule is that a horse first must be able to canter well in a pure three-beat rhythm. The canter should have good elevation and energy, and be controlled. The canter should already be somewhat collected and really give the impression of being uphill. A horse should be able to counter-canter in both directions with ease. He should have a command of the simple changes through the walk, and he should be able to do effortless tempo changes in the canter in both directions. If everything I described is in order, then your horse meets the basic requirements for doing a flying change."

"In my experience," van Baalen says, "you really get a lot of control and obedience mainly by doing simple changes on a diagonal or another straight line. I think it's a perfect preparation for changes for many horses."

How

In the canter, the rider should always feel like he's continually repeating the canter aids. The rider's inside leg maintains the canter, as though he wants to begin to canter all over again; the outside leg stays back a little to control the hindquarters. The rider makes the horse attentive when doing a change by half-halting, that is, through the short, simultaneous effect of his driving, seat, and rein aids. The actual aid for the change is given shortly before the moment of suspension. The rider holds his upper body still and moves his outside leg, which is positioned slightly back, forward to the girth and his original inside leg a bit back behind the girth. This change in the position of the rider's legs will automatically slightly push forward his new inside hip. The horse is slightly bent in the new direction. The rider should give the new inside rein a little so that the inside hind leg can sufficiently stride through and forward. "This is often where things go wrong!" van Baalen warns. "Riders often forget to give the inside rein."

The rider must maintain a light connection with the horse's mouth. For most horses, the left lead canter is easier than the right lead canter. Therefore, we recommend doing the first change from right to left. Furthermore, in the beginning, it is helpful with many horses to always do the change at the same spot in the arena until they completely understand what the rider wants and can do the change there without

Olympic Ferro and Coby van Baalen doing a nicely executed change in Aachen, 1998.

any problem. That particular spot should preferably be on a straight line, as changes on curved lines require more balance from the horse. Changes on curved lines are reserved for more advanced horses. "If I consider the aids this way," says van Baalen, "I naturally have to talk about them separately, although all the aids obviously go hand-in-hand in practice."

"First of all," continues Hinnemann, "I want to emphasize that the rider always must concentrate when giving the aids. A rider who wants to ask for a change must concentrate very hard on changing to the other lead. The rider's aids should reflect that as well. A rider can develop feel for the timing and application of aids by getting experience on a schoolmaster that can do changes easily. A rider should also definitely learn to forego doing a change at pre-planned spot if one of the prerequisites is not in order, such as the contact. Ride on, reorganize, and get your horse on the aids again."

Straightness even plays a part in the flying changes, as Commodore correctly demonstrates in the picture, Münster, 1992.

Frequency

In the beginning, it is certainly fine to do only one or two changes in the easier direction and be content with that. "The rider who takes time teaching the changes will be rewarded," says Hinnemann. "Don't do flying changes everyday; continue doing lots of tempo changes in the canter and simple changes through the walk. Those are exercises that improve the horse in general and reap benefits later for the changes. Furthermore, every horse has a different reaction time to the aids. The rider knows his horse's reaction time and should consider this in applying the aids at the correct moment. One horse may need more time than the another."

Preparations

Every rider should try to discover the easiest method and the best place for his horse to execute a change. Some methods that seem complicated are actually the simplest in practice. "Good preparation is always necessary," insists van Baalen. "I always ask my students to do lots of tempo changes and canter-walk-canter transitions to get their horses really on the leg and attentive to the aids. Decreasing and increasing a circle in a travers-like position in the canter, and then riding forward on the circle, also gets the horse nicely on the aids. Decreasing the circle makes the horse collect; increasing the circle maintains the impulsion and forwardness. The idea behind all of this is to get the horse optimally on the aids and to allow him to canter nicely uphill. Furthermore, the hind legs must stay under the horse."

Cantering in a somewhat shoulder-in position on the circle also helps to keep the horse's hind legs underneath him. "A rider should be inventive," van Baalen says. "He should sense the kind of preparations his horse needs in order to canter energetically and to stay on the aids well, making a correctly executed change possible."

Methods

There are various ways to begin flying changes on a green horse. "One thing though," Hinnemann warns, "never start changes over a ground pole. Most horses will jump over it with a high croup, which really invites the horse to change late; in other words, the horse changes in front and then behind."

The following method seems to be the easiest way for horses to do their first change: The rider canters the horse on the second track with the tempo not too collected. Then, the rider asks for the change to the counter canter. "The rider has the whole long side of the second track to give the aids," says Hinnemann. "If the horse doesn't respond right away, then the rider can quietly repeat the aids. The horse won't run off quickly because he does the change toward the track. Furthermore, this exercise also confirms the counter-canter so, as his training progresses, the horse will be less likely to change on his own to the true canter."

Another well-known line for doing the first flying change is cantering a relatively large half-circle at A or C to the right or left, on which the rider gives the aids for the change before the horse reaches the track.

"This line is especially useful for a rider who has to learn changes on a schoolmaster—a horse that already knows how to do them," says van Baalen. "The rider can concentrate and target the exact spot where he should give the aids for the change."

Horses that can already do canter half-passes usually do not have difficulty doing a change as they approach the track after doing a canter half-pass from the centerline or quarter-line. "There is some danger of the horse running off or not changing clean," says Hinnemann, "especially with horses that aren't balanced enough. They lose a lot of jump and impulsion during the half-pass, and therefore can't do the change correctly."

Mistakes

The mistakes most often made in doing changes are a lack of response to the aids and not changing cleanly. "A horse that is learning changes should never be punished if he doesn't respond to the aids for the change or doesn't change cleanly," Hinneman says. "In that case, the rider shouldn't go on endlessly trying to get a change, but instead, he should go back to improving the prerequisites for the change. He should go back to doing tempo changes in the canter and simple changes through the walk until he feels that his horse is on the aids again. Then he can try a flying change again, though 'again' can also be the next day or the next week."

Van Baalen adds, "As the canter goes, so the change goes. If the canter isn't in order, then you can't expect the change to be in order either."

The rider may also be the cause of an incorrect change. Riders who do not sit quietly enough can disturb the horse's balance which can result in the horse changing incorrectly. Riders who block the horse with the inside hand do not give the horse the opportunity to jump forward energetically. Riders who give the aids late restrict the horse as well. "I very often have my students ride without stirrups and practice changes without stirrups," Hinneman asserts. "As far as I'm concerned, Coby can ride without stirrups just about every day, even if we're training at the Olympic Games! A balanced rider can sit so quietly and supplely that he can also effortlessly ask for flying changes without stirrups. However, you often see riders whose seats come too far out of the saddle. The horse reacts to that by not changing cleanly. In that case, the rider needs to do a lot of work to learn how to give smaller aids and to sit more quietly. On dressage protocols, I'd like not only to see the statement 'effectiveness of the aids' but also 'invisibility of the aids.' This is essential for not disturbing the horse's balance and allowing him to perform everything to the best of his ability."

Sometimes horses change late in front rather than behind. "This is usually easier to correct than a horse that changes late behind," says Hinnemann. "Here's the remedy: Make the horse canter energetically forward, uphill; prepare him well for the change, using precise aids; and really pay attention that you give the new inside hand sufficiently at the moment of the change."

"It can also make a difference where you ask for the change," van Baalen adds. "For instance, if you ask for the change in the corner at the end of a diagonal line, then the horse can do a clean change more easily."

Some horses are very crooked in their changes, which usually has to do with a rider who applies the lateral driving aids too strongly when switching leg position. It may also be that the horse is overbent. "Sometimes horses that are crooked in changes hold themselves tight and don't accept the rider's forward driving aids enough," says Hinnemann. "The horse isn't sufficiently in front of the rider's leg. In this case, too,

The complete picture of a flying change should radiate "nice riding" and present a content horse.

Marlies van Baalen on Inspekteur, and Coby van Baalen on More Magic, in the same phase of a correctly executed flying change to the right.

the rider should go back to doing tempo changes and transitions until the horse is on the forward aids again. It can also be helpful to think about the best place in the arena to ask for a change. With a horse whose changes are crooked, that place just may be on the track and preferably doing the change from the true canter to the counter-canter."

Sometimes, horses have bad experiences with their first attempts at doing a flying change, and subsequent attempts then result in the horse running off. "I've continually said that, before attempting a change, the foundation of an energetic, uphill canter has to be in order," Hinnemann says emphatically. "The foundation consists of a straight horse that goes on the contact, that is obedient, and that is on the driving aids. If that's not the case, then the rider needs to school the horse again by doing a lot of tempo changes and transitions. With horses that run off, it's helpful to change to counter-canter on the track or the second track. It's also helpful to do a lot of simple changes so that the horse doesn't know what to expect. Alternating simple changes with flying changes on a serpentine can also help the horse concentrate and prevent him from running through the aids."

More Expression

A good flying change demonstrates uphill, energetic jump, and expression. However, Hinnemann can offer advice on how to make a good flying change even better. It all comes down to stimulating the hindquarters to really bear weight while maintaining the horse's energy and impulsion. "First do a change on a circle from the counter-canter to the true canter," he says. "In the counter-canter, the rider encourages the inside hind leg to really stride through. If the horse canters energetically, then the rider can ask for the change as he touches the track, for example. The rider has to ensure that he gives sufficiently with the new inside rein

The phases of the right lead canter.

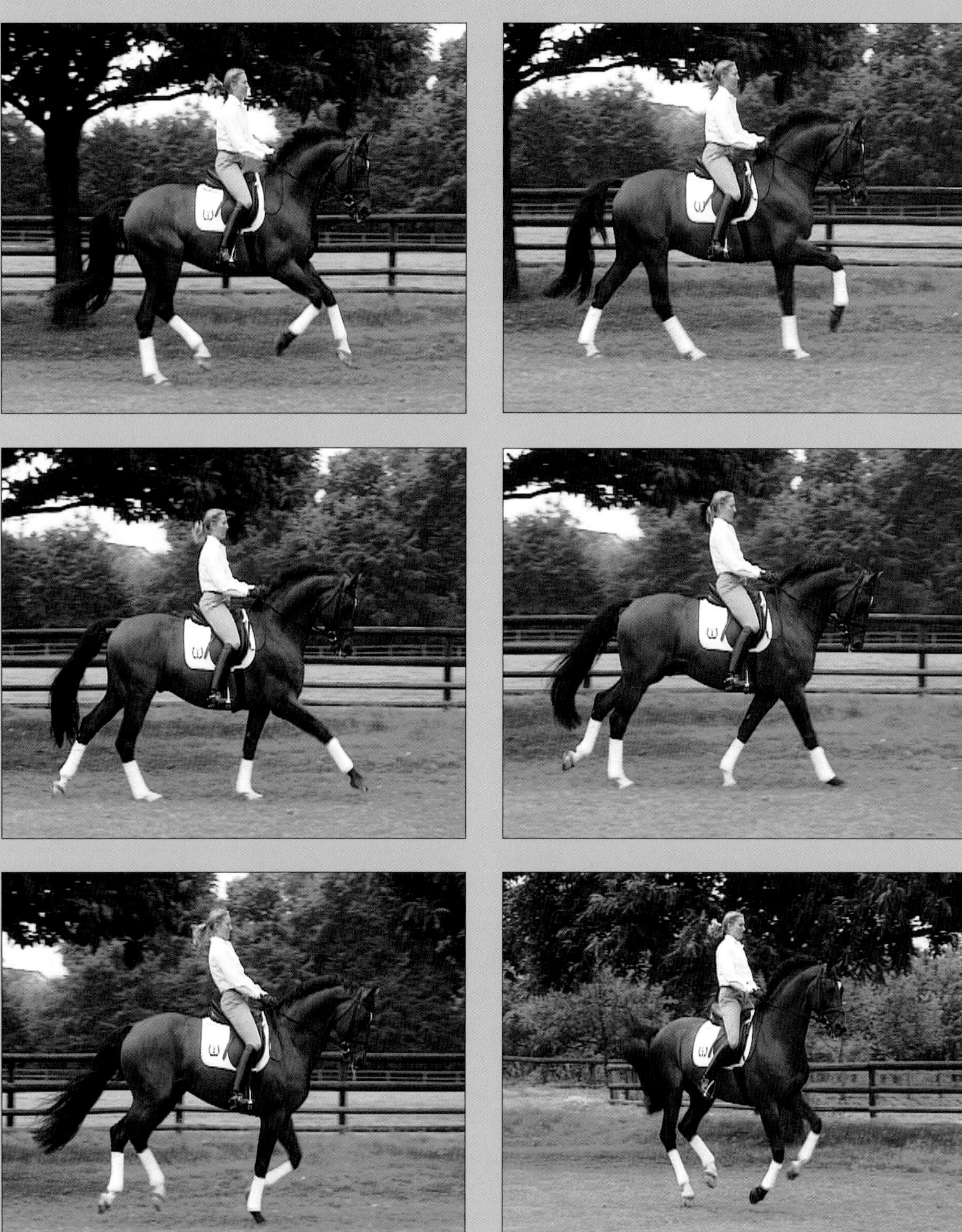

The horse can only do a flying change during the moment of suspension, the sixth phase. Marlies van Baalen on Idocus.

The phases of the left lead canter.

See Chapter Three on rhythm for a complete description of the correct footfalls in the canter.

The rider's aids during the flying change.

The change to the right. Notice the rider's inside leg aid (right leg).

The same change to the right. The rider's outside leg aid (left leg) is visible.

The change to the left. Notice the rider's inside leg aid (left leg).

The same change to the left. The rider's outside leg aid (right leg) is visible.

"Sometimes a horse will hold his breath during the changes," says Hinnemann. "Sooner or later this will cause problems; however, preventing something like this is difficult. In such a case, you have to continually emphasize relaxation during the changes, both internal and external losgelassenheit. You should also avoid progressing too quickly to riding a series of changes; instead, go back several steps to riding simple changes."

to also allow the new inside hind leg enough room to jump through." "I think doing changes on a circle is a really nice exercise," adds van Baalen. "Doing changes on a circle forces the rider to better prepare and to concentrate on the aids, which he must give more precisely. Horses often get straighter in their changes by riding on a circle. The circle is also a good place for horses that tend to do a change before the rider gives the aids. In that case, it's best to do the changes from the true canter to the counter-canter."

Another way to give the flying changes more expression is by including working pirouettes. The rider begins the working pirouette, decreases it in a travers-like position, and decreases it again. At the moment he feels the horse really starts to bear weight on his hindquarters, he canters a diagonal line from the pirouette, asks the horse for a nice, uphill change, and goes on the circle in the other direction to start another working pirouette. "This method really teaches the horse to nicely execute his changes with an uphill tendency," explains Hinnemann. "Furthermore, it develops both sides of the horse equally and gymnasticizes him on both reins. Horses also learn not to run off or hold themselves too tightly in the changes. Tightness, or loss of *losgelassenheit*, should never be the result of an exercise. These things prevent the correct execution of any movement."

On the Way to a Series

A rider should obviously not attempt successive changes until the horse does single changes in both directions without problems and successfully responds to the rider's every request for a change. The horse should do changes from the true canter to the counter-canter as easily as he does changes from the counter-canter to the true canter. "In order to reach that point, the rider must develop a sufficient feel for the aids and for doing the changes," says Hinnemann.

Hinnemann and van Baalen usually prepare for a series of flying changes by cantering the horse on the second track and doing two changes on the long side: to the counter-canter and back again. "The number of canter strides in between each change is unimportant," emphasizes van Baalen. "Whether it happens after five or ten canter strides, it's only important that the horse is straight again after the first change and is well on the aids for the second change." Riders do not usually experience difficulty getting two changes on the long side. Then the rider can try for three by starting in the counter-canter and changing to the true canter, and then returning to the counter-canter and then the true canter again. As before, the number of canter strides in between changes is not important. "The horse must stay straight and continue to canter energetically without becoming tense now that the aids are being applied in quicker succession," says Hinnemann. "This brings us to the demands that are placed on the rider."

The Rider

For an inexperienced rider, the most difficult aspect of flying changes is usually concentrating on giving the correct aids at the right time. "Coby and I have said several times that every inexperienced rider should be able to develop his feel on an experienced horse," says Hinnemann. "Even then, it's difficult enough. However, I can give the rider some concentration techniques. I think variety in the work is very important. For example, after doing three successive changes on the long side, you can do a few simple changes on the next long side before doing several flying changes again on the long side of the second track. The simple changes force the rider to really concentrate on the aids for changing to the other lead, aids that the rider also uses for the flying changes. I also have riders do six canter strides in shoulder-in after a change and then have them do another change, for example. That also improves the rider's concentration for giving the correct aids. Furthermore, using an exact number of canter strides helps facilitate riding an extended change series with an exact number of canter strides."

"Of course," van Baalen adds, "the rider should apply finer and less noticeable aids as the horse becomes more schooled and confirmed. Riders who school many young horses and teach them changes often aren't able refine their aids. These riders should ride without stirrups more often so they can learn to sit more quietly in the changes and keep their seats firmly in the saddle."

The First Series

Once a rider and his horse can do three changes on the long side, the pair will often advance quite quickly. It will also seem like these three changes are not too difficult to ride in an exact number of canter strides; for example, in six or five or four canter strides.

"You're sometimes amazed at how quickly this part of the training progresses," Hinnemann says. "In one week, a horse and rider team will do a flawless series of three canter strides, with five changes in a row. The rider should especially concentrate on giving the aids at the right time and counting in his head. In a series of four changes, I always use the word 'and' instead of 'four,' mainly to keep the forward energy in mind. For a series of four changes, for example, you count 'one-two-three and two-two-three and three-two-three and four-two-three and five-two-three.' That way, you have immediately counted the number of changes, and the 'and' helps you concentrate on the aids for the next change so that you're always on time."

Not on the Diagonal

When first schooling them, Hinnemann and van Baalen expressly avoid riding a series of changes on the diagonal. "That is asking for problems, such as not staying straight," says van Baalen. "The horse may also swing from left to right or run off. Riding on the second track gives you support from the wall. Once a horse becomes accustomed to swinging back and forth in the changes, it's difficult to teach him to stop."

A rider should only ask for a series of changes on the diagonal when the change series on the second track is well confirmed. "A dressage test that includes a series of five changes every fourth stride, for example, also requires that the changes be evenly divided over the diagonal," van Baalen continues. "The middle change of this series of five changes, which is the third one, should be done approximately at X. This requires the rider to know how big his horse's stride is. He has to estimate at which point on the diagonal to do his first change."

Ones

Riding changes every stride is an art in itself. Of course, a logical progression requires that one-tempi changes are attempted only after the two-tempi changes are well confirmed. Nevertheless, Hinnemann somewhat deviates from this in practice with young horses that can do changes easily. "I often prepare four- or five-year-olds that can do changes easily for the one-tempi changes by practicing 'left-right': changing and then immediately changing back," he says. "I repeat this a couple of times so that the horse remembers the exercise."

When the horse is older, Hinnemann goes back to this "left-right" on the "one-two." Horses that have yet to learn one-tempi changes are first confirmed again by riding two successive changes. "I practice those until they become second nature," Hinnemann says. "Then, I also do the 'one-two' in a series: change-change, three canter strides, then change-change again, three canter strides, then one-two again, and so on. I do that in both directions."

If this is also successful, then two series of "one-two" are done successively. "Above all, if the horse makes mistakes or has problems with the ones, the rider should not get angry or punish the horse," stresses Hinneman. "Creating extra tension by punishing the horse is counter-productive to the one-tempi changes. Don't underestimate how much is demanded of the horse's ability to react and dependent on his obedient response to the aids. Some horses learn the two-tempis without a single problem yet feel stressed when asked for the ones. That's when the rider needs a lot of patience. In addition, he needs to consider what he can still improve about his own riding in order to increase his horse's sensitivity to the aids, as well as to be able to return to the 'one-twos.' He can try to build again from this point."

One-tempi changes should be done in a collected tempo, especially at first. "In general," van Baalen says, "horses find one-tempis easier to do when in a collected tempo. Also, there's a significant danger of the rider not applying the aids at the right time when riding at a faster tempo. However, as soon as the horse's one-tempis are somewhat confirmed, he should be ridden forward again in addition to being ridden collected. The ultimate goal is for the horse to do changes with impulsion, reach, and in an uphill attitude, even in the ones."

Losgelassenheit

Finally, van Baalen and Hinnemann emphasize the complete picture, which should radiate "nice riding." With this image, the six principles that are the main theme in this book come full circle. Hinnemann describes his idea of "nice riding" as follows: "The total picture has to be in order. The horse canters 'uphill' and appears active but calm. The poll should be the highest point with the nose in front of the vertical. In addition, the horse is totally straight and content in his work. I'd like to use the same word with which we started this book: *losgelassen.* This includes internal and external relaxation and contentment. Actually, relaxation is not entirely the right word; the intention is that the horse should not use his muscles beyond what is required."

A memorable and emotional moment during the Olympic Games in Sydney: The team enters, preceding the grooms, to receive the honors and awards for the Olympic International Dressage Competition. From left to right: Ellen Bontje on Silvano N, Anky van Grunsven on Bonfire, Arjen Teeuwissen on Goliath T, and Coby van Baalen on Olympic Ferro.

Recommended Reading

"*Reiten lernt man nur durch reiten;* you learn to ride only by riding," Johann Hinnemann says, quoting a well-known expression. However, he immediately follows that by saying, "I agree that you learn to ride only by riding, but theory and logical thought are inextricably bound to riding. One doesn't go without the other!"

Riders cannot progress without theory. They must learn to think logically and to know exactly why they do something. "A rider should constantly analyze what he feels from his horse," says Hinnemann. "He should concentrate and formulate a plan before he gets in the saddle. He should get feedback from his instructor on what he feels when in the saddle. He should consider the new instructions he receives and strive to engage them in a harmonious way with how his horse feels, just as his instructor considers the scores he receives from a judge, reconciles these scores with how his horse feels, and uses that feedback in training."

One should keep riding and practicing, but also read, and think about what one reads. Books on riding occupy many shelves of Hinnemann's home in Voerde, Germany. On occasion, he still consults an old master. "We are keeping things simple, as we promised at the beginning of this book," Hinneman says. "This book contains the complete theory on how to learn to ride well, and of course, I recommend it from my heart. The two German National Equestrian Federation texts, deal with riding theory a bit more in depth. In addition, every dressage rider's education should include studying Boldt and Steinbrecht. I have included the late Dr. Reiner Klimke's book, champion several times over, because I began as a rider with him."

The Dressage Horse, Harry Boldt: (*Das Dressur Pferd*, Edition Haberbeck, 1978), Chapter Three available in English through Knight Equestrian Books (US).

Ahlerich: The Making of a Dressage World Champion, Dr. Reiner Klimke: (*Ahlerich, von der Remonte bis zum Dressurweltmeister*, ein exemplarischer Ausbildingsweg, Frankische verlagshandlung Stuttgart, 2nd edition, 1985), English translation out-of-print, some copies available but extremely rare, Half Halt Press (US) and Merehurst Press (UK).

Principles of Riding, German National Equestrian Federation: (*Richtlinien für Reiten und Fahren Band I, Grundausbildung*, FN-Verlag der Deutschen Reiterlichen Vereinigung, Warendorf, 26th edition, 1994), available in English through Half Halt Press (US) and Kenilworth Press (UK).

Advanced Techniques of Dressage, German National Equestrian Federation: (*Richtlinien für Reiten und Fahren Band II, Ausbildung für Fortegeschrittenen*, FN-Verlag der Deutschen Reiterlichen Vereinigung, Warendorf, 12th edition, 1997), available in English through Half Halt Press (US) and Kenilworth Press (UK).

The Gymnasium of the Horse, Gustav Steinbrecht: (*Das Gymnasium des Pferdes*, Cadmos, revised edition, 1998, 1st edition, 1884), available in English through Xenophon Press (US).

Index

Page numbers in *italics* indicate illustrations.

Illustration Credits

Photographs in this book were taken mainly by the following photographers:

Arnd Bronkhorst, Dirk Caremans, Ellen van Leeuwen & Jacob Melissen.

Other photographers include:
Claartje van Andel, Arie van Baalen, Marjan Dorresteijn, Werner Ernst, Bernd Eylers, Karl-Heinz Frieler, Heribert Herbertz, Maarten Jurgens, Julia Körber, Paard & Foto, Video Reichel, Henriette Rootveld, Studio Temps de Roses, Janneke Teeuwen, Ruud van Tienen, Sandra Nieuwendijk, Arjen Veldt, Rijk van Vulpen, Glen Wassenberg & Dorli Welp.

The drawings in this book were reprinted with permission from:

Principles of Riding, German National Equestrian Federation (*Richtlinien für Reiten und Fahren Band I, Grundausbildung*, FN-Verlag der Deutschen Reiterlichen Vereinigung, Warendorf, 1994, 26th edition.)